The

SECRET

OF THE

SEVEN SEEDS

DAVID FISCHMAN

A PARABLE *of* LEADERSHIP AND LIFE

The SECRET OF THE SEVEN SEEDS

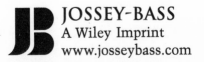

JOSSEY-BASS
A Wiley Imprint
www.josseybass.com

Published by Jossey-Bass
A Wiley Imprint
989 Market Street, San Francisco, CA 94103-1741   www.josseybass.com

Translated from Spanish by Pat Courtney.

Readers should be aware that Internet Web sites offered as citations and/or sources for
further information may have changed or disappeared between the time this was written
and when it is read.

Jossey-Bass books and products are available through most bookstores. To contact Jossey-Bass
directly call our Customer Care Department within the U.S. at 800-956-7739, outside the
U.S. at 317-572-3986, or fax 317-572-4002.

Jossey-Bass also publishes its books in a variety of electronic formats. Some content that
appears in print may not be available in electronic books.

Library of Congress Cataloging-in-Publication Data

Fischman, David, 1958-
   [Secreto de las siete semillas. English]
   The secret of the seven seeds : a parable of leadership and life / by David Fischman.
      p. cm.
   ISBN-13: 978-0-7879-8461-8 (cloth)
   ISBN-10: 0-7879-8461-2 (cloth)
  1. Success—Religious aspects. 2. Success in business—Religious aspects.
3. Leadership—Religious aspects. I. Title.
   BL65.S84F5713 2006
   294.3'444—dc22

                                        2006005269

Printed in the United States of America
FIRST EDITION
HB Printing   10 9 8 7 6 5 4 3 2 1

CONTENTS

FOREWORD

The "great Western disease" is rapidly spreading around the world. The disease is called, "I will be happy when . . ." *When I get that money, when I get that racy car, when I get that new house, when I get that promotion.*

In the United States people have more money than ever. They live in bigger houses, they have achieved record levels of productivity, and they have not increased happiness. Depression is at an all-time high! I was just in Shanghai. In the faces of amazingly hard-working young leaders, I could see this same hunger for *things*—and the same mistaken belief that these *things* would lead to happiness and contentment. I see this same hunger—and this same mistaken belief—in the faces of working professionals around the world.

As you read *The Secret of the Seven Seeds,* think of the master's first question—"Are you happy?"

If your answer is, "Not as much as I would like to be," then you—like Ignacio—may need to consider walking down a new path in life. You may want to look in the mirror and thoughtfully assess your true satisfaction with the person who is looking back at you.

In my speaking to large groups, I usually ask this question: "How many of you feel under as much pressure today as you have ever felt in your lives?" About 80 percent of the people in the room raise their hands. In the "old days" many professional jobs required thirty-five to forty hours of work a week and came with four-week vacations. Those days are gone. Global capitalism has created incredible expectations and demands. With personal computers, laptops, PDAs, and cell phones, many of the professionals that I meet live in a 24/7 world of work. In the old days if you were not happy at work but had a huge amount of time off, it was easier to rationalize the sacrifice. If you are in a demanding professional job today—and you are not happy—you may be living in that unpleasant place that I call *new-age professional hell.*

In my work as an executive coach, my mission is to help highly successful leaders achieve a positive, measurable change in behavior. For most of us, positive behavioral change at work leads to positive behavioral change at home. Although David does not address the issue of family in the book, the same changes that help us at work can help us at home. Many leaders I meet, like Ignacio in the beginning of the book, are impatient, stubborn, and opinionated. If we are impatient, stubborn, and opinionated at work, it is highly unlikely that we become notably patient and open-minded when we go home! Changes that make us better professionals often make us better parents, spouses, partners, or friends.

As you read *The Secret of the Seven Seeds,* think about the lessons that you can apply in your own life.

I am a Buddhist. As a Buddhist I have a mission to help you have a happier life. Buddha believed that we should use only those teachings that help us achieve happiness and contentment in our own lives. Ask yourself, What teachings from this book can I apply to achieve greater happiness and contentment in my own life?

Don't worry about being *perfect*—or doing *everything*—that is suggested. Don't make yourself feel guilty for what you haven't done in the past. We cannot change the past. We can change the future!

If you can incorporate one change from the teachings in this book—one change that helps you have a better life—this will be one of the most valuable books that you have ever read.

Challenge yourself as you read. Don't evaluate the book—evaluate yourself. Ask yourself one question as you read, How can I use what I am learning to create a better life for myself—and for the people I meet?

You can do it!

March 2006   Marshall Goldsmith

The
SECRET
OF THE
SEVEN SEEDS

CHAPTER ONE

Wake-Up Call

Ignacio Rodríguez was anxiously awaiting his turn at the cardiologist's. At forty-two years of age, he still couldn't believe that he had heart trouble. He had always been a healthy man. Lately he had been working eighteen hours a day, Monday through Saturday, stopping only to sleep. He had neglected his children, his wife, and his body. He never did any exercise. He drank and smoked too much. He ate mostly fast food, because he often had lunch at the office while he was working.

He still remembered the day his father died. Before dying, don José asked him to take on the general management of R & G, a large family import business. José Rodríguez had built R & G into the market leader and now Ignacio had the responsibility of keeping the firm in that position. But things had become complicated. He felt like one of those surfers who row with their arms against the tide to get out among the waves, but don't manage to go far enough out to sea. The waves of change affecting R & G were so strong that with each wave he was thrown farther back than the progress he had made, and he found himself in a vicious circle of effort and exhaustion.

Deregulation and globalization had opened the way for large companies, with economies of scale, to establish themselves in the country. There were price wars and increased competition in a now-smaller market affected by the recession. The few national competitors who were left were forming alliances with transnationals. R & G was the only company working alone with domestic capital. The increase in competition had struck at the worst possible time. For two years now the balance sheets had been recording losses and the company was in debt. The banks had cut off the firm's credit and some had even started legal action to recover their loans. The last days of the month were torture for Ignacio, because he often didn't have money available to pay his workers. He had already reduced staff twice, but this was still not enough to balance the books.

The atmosphere at R & G was tense and full of uncertainty. Employees were unmotivated and talked among themselves about how different things had been when don José was managing the company. They had lost their confidence in Ignacio and they looked back with nostalgia to the times when the company had been successful.

Just one week earlier, the sales manager had handed in his letter of resignation, admitting that he was going over to the competition for twice the salary. Ignacio had been furious, shouting and insulting the man, but in the middle of it all he had felt a very sharp pain in his chest, under the sternum. He felt pressure on his chest and his left arm went numb. Then he felt very agitated and found that he couldn't breathe properly, and he fainted. Hours later, in the clinic, they told him that he had

had an attack of angina pectoris, commonly known as a heart attack, and he was very lucky to be alive. At his age, a high percentage of people with heart conditions lose their lives.

A week after the incident, Ignacio felt so well that he really thought he was wasting his time waiting to see the doctor. Three days in the clinic had been more than enough to fill him with anxiety to get back to the company to sort out the backlog of work.

At last the doctor showed him into his office. He first confirmed Ignacio's optimism.

"Surprising!" he said. "Your heart has recovered faster than normal."

Ignacio sprang up from his chair.

"Great! Now, Doctor, I think it's time I was back in the office to deal with my work—"

"Not so fast," said the doctor sternly, taking hold of his arm. "Take this seriously, Ignacio. You must understand that you have two possibilities: if you go on living an unbalanced life, with constant anxiety and stress, I give you only a few more years before a fatal heart attack. But if you make a radical change in your lifestyle, you'll have a healthier, longer life. It's your decision. You'd better take care of yourself. It is very risky to have a heart attack at your age. I don't have statistics of deaths from heart attacks in age groups, but from my own experience with my patients, at your age approximately half of the patients who have a heart attack die."

"Oh, come on, don't exaggerate!" said Ignacio, looking at the doctor with a gesture of incredulity. "You've seen how quickly I've gotten over it. Don't worry, I'm made of steel and I'm going to be around a long time yet. Now please excuse me;

I must get back to the company to prevent any greater evils. You can never really relax when your subordinates are running the show."

The doctor looked at him indulgently, as if Ignacio were a child who was incapable of seeing the mistakes he was making.

"Look, Ignacio, you are free to decide what to do with your life. If you choose to die, that's your decision. But please stop thinking so much about yourself and think of your children. You have two little kids. Don't let them lose their father at their age. That would mark them for life."

"OK," said Ignacio and he sat down again with resignation. "What do I have to do?"

The doctor suggested that he lead a more balanced life and start eating a healthy diet; he asked him to give up smoking, and if he drank liquor, to do so in moderation; and he told him to reduce the pace of his work and the stress.

"Doctor, I can do all that; but what I can't help and can't control are the problems in the office, the aggressive behavior of the competition, the company's lack of money, and the recession."

"Right," replied the doctor, "but what you can control is your reaction to those stimuli. You need to relax and learn to have a different perspective on life. Have you heard of meditation?"

"Sorry, Doctor, but I don't believe in any of those esoteric things," answered Ignacio somewhat complacently. "My wife is into that kind of thing. I find it ridiculous."

While he spoke, Ignacio looked at his watch and shifted in his seat as if he did not fit into it. The doctor felt that the only way to convince him was to get directly to the point.

"Ignacio, the subject of meditation is no longer considered esoteric. It has even been researched by very serious universities. Dr. Benson, of Harvard, mentions a study about the effects of meditation on Buddhist monks in Tibet.[1] The results were astonishing. The human body has a mechanism called the fight-or-flight response, which dates back to when we human beings lived in caves. In those times, when we perceived a threatening stimulus, such as the roar of a wild animal, we would automatically prepare to fight or run away. The hypothalamus, a gland near the brain, orchestrated a whole physiological reaction. Even now, the human heart beats faster when we are threatened, to pump more blood into our arms and legs; our breathing is quicker, the blood moves out of the stomach to protect the weakest part of the body, and adrenaline and cortisol are produced to keep us on high alert."

The doctor paused to see whether his words were having any effect. Then he went on:

"Our problem nowadays is that we continue to perceive threatening stimuli: economic or family crises, problems at the office . . . and we still automatically activate the fight-or-flight response. It was different at the time of the cavemen, when the threatening stimuli were sporadic; but today we are continually under threat. And worse still, since the threats are psychological, we don't have to run away or to fight with anybody. As a result, we have no physical exercise, which is vital to minimize the effects of these chemicals in our body. Quite the opposite— and this is true of practically all executives—the excessive

---

[1] H. Benson, with M. Z. Klipper, *The Relaxation Response*. New York: Avon Books, 2000, p. 47.

amount of work makes us cut out physical exercise altogether. This means that your body is constantly receiving hormones and chemicals that you fail to discharge and that overstimulates you, causing stress and all kinds of aches and pains."

Ignacio continued to look incredulous. He kept looking at his watch.

"See here, Ignacio," continued the doctor, "it's as if your body were a car in neutral and you had your foot on the gas: you're not moving, and yet you're accelerating to the equivalent of 150 kilometers per hour. Most of us do that these days. We spend our whole lives accelerating the car in neutral every time we perceive a threat. That is why, when we want to go for a ride, we'll find that the engine's blown. The typical consequence of living permanently in this state is a blown engine; that is, hypertension and heart problems. The study of the Buddhist monks cited by Dr. Benson revealed that the same gland, the hypothalamus, that's responsible for the fight-or-flight response also produces a reverse mechanism, the relaxation response, as a result of meditation.[2] The doctor found that when the monks entered a state of meditation, their heartbeat, their breathing, and their consumption of oxygen slowed down, and they felt a sensation of peace and tranquility. Ignacio, what you need to do is to teach your own body to eliminate the effects of stress."

"Well, thanks a lot, Doctor," said Ignacio. He strung together a couple of excuses and superfluous comments, and left.

The comment about meditation had been intriguing. However, Ignacio was not fully convinced. It was one of the things

[2] Benson with Klipper, p. 73.

that his wife, Miriam, was keen on, and that he had always considered a fraud, a kind of hobby for upper-class ladies who had time on their hands.

At home, when he told Miriam about the doctor's recommendations, she couldn't hide her enthusiasm:

"Ignacio, how wonderful that you're going to try meditation at last! It'll do you a world of good! I know of an Indian master who lives in Surquillo."

Miriam handed him a piece of paper with a name and address on it. Ignacio put it in his wallet, without showing much interest. He thought: "You needn't think I'm going to be doing the same silly things you do. I can't go around wasting my time."

∼⟨⟩∽

A month had gone by since the heart attack and Ignacio felt fine. As far as he was concerned, his illness was over and done with. There were still problems, but . . . who didn't have problems nowadays? He had stopped drinking and smoking in excess and felt very proud of himself for doing that.

That morning, when he reached his office, the head of corporate sales told him they had lost their biggest account. The largest department store in the country was going to stop buying from them and work with their closest competitor. Ignacio began shouting at the sales officer, insulting him, and telling him it was all his fault. In the middle of his tirade, he started feeling a slight pain in his chest again. He sat down, scared, and stopped shouting. He tried to calm down, and gradually managed to get back to normal. He realized that life was sending him a last warning, and there would be no more. If he didn't make an effort to reduce his stress, his life was on the line.

He remembered that he had the address of the guru in his wallet. He took it out, fumbling in his desperation to find it. He picked up his jacket and set off to Surquillo.

The master's house looked humble but attractive. It had white walls and a large blue door, neatly painted. Because it was clean and well maintained, it stuck out in the neighborhood like an oasis. Ignacio hesitated outside the house; he didn't know whether to knock at the door or not. What the hell was he doing standing here? He had never, in all his life, visited a fortune-teller, clairvoyant, or guru. He was a professional businessman, very rational, and he did not believe in these weird things. Still, that sensation of suffocation had frightened him; he realized that he must do something for his health before it was too late. He knocked and was let in.

On the other side of the door he found a well-tended garden with a great variety of flowers and fruit trees. Entering this house was like coming to a different world; a kind of Shangri-La in the middle of Surquillo. The house was set back from the street some 20 meters, and the garden stretched between the street entrance and the front of the house. Beside the front door of the house were six wicker chairs. Sitting there were four people, talking. They stopped talking when they saw Ignacio and looked at him as if he were a being from another planet. Ignacio felt as if he had been cut up into little pieces. "How embarrassing! Whatever must they think of me!" he said to himself. "A businessman like me . . . consulting shamans! It'll just take one of them to recognize me, or turn out to be the wife of a friend of mine, for the whole business community to find out and then I'll be the laughingstock!"

Ignacio sat at the other end of the garden. While he waited, he noticed huge ferns and a row of bonsais against one of the side walls, but what most caught his attention was the great variety of the plants—practically no two were the same. Despite the pleasant surroundings, he started imagining all kinds of catastrophes. They might come from a television channel to interview the "shaman" and he, Ignacio, would come out on all the news programs. . . . Finally, a young man approached and took him inside.

The house had a strong smell of incense. The walls were hung with pictures of half-naked individuals sitting in the lotus position. Ignacio followed his guide into a room where there was a man who looked about seventy years old, with a white beard and thick eyebrows. He was slim and brown-skinned, and was dressed in a salmon-colored tunic. He was sitting on some white cushions. On the wall behind him hung about a dozen pictures. One larger one stood out from the others: it was the photo of another man in a tunic, and he looked about a hundred years old. In other small frames there were photos of still other men with bare torsos. There were also pictures with drawings of gods of some Oriental religion. Several candles were burning on the altar.

The master silently motioned for him to sit on a cushion. Then he gazed into his eyes for a few seconds. While the master looked at him, he said nothing. Ignacio felt completely out of place. "When will this weird man start speaking? Is he dumb?" he wondered, as he silently cursed the hour it had occurred to him to come here. At last the master spoke:

"What is your name?"

"Ignacio Rodríguez."

"What brings you here?"

"I want you to teach me to relax, what you call meditation."

The master was silent again. He merely gazed into his eyes. Ignacio was most uncomfortable. He felt that this look went right through him. He didn't know whether to stand up and go or sit and stay. After some minutes of silence, which seemed hours to Ignacio, the master again asked him:

"What have you come for?"

"Like I said, I want you to teach me relaxation!" Ignacio spoke louder to show that besides wasting time, he had also lost his patience.

The master remained silent a few minutes more. Ignacio felt attacked by the master's silence. "What's wrong with this idiot?" he thought. "Is he deaf?" He was used to action. Time was gold, and he felt he was wasting it.

Finally the man spoke again, this time as if he knew something that Ignacio was not even capable of glimpsing:

"That is not the real reason that brings you here. Tell me, Ignacio Rodríguez, why have you come if you really do not believe that I can help you?"

"That's exactly what I was wondering myself!" replied Ignacio indignantly. "In fact I think this has been a ridiculous waste of time," he added as he picked up his jacket. "Go on tricking rich women who believe in your every word just because you're from India. As far as I'm concerned, you're a charlatan."

Ignacio strode quickly to the door of the room. When he was near the door, the master asked him softly:

"Tell me, are you happy?"

Ignacio felt those words were stabbing him in the center of his back. He suddenly felt like physically assaulting the old man, but he kept himself under control. What right did this man have to tell him he was unhappy? On top of having to take so much aggression at work, he now had to support it here in this little cubbyhole. But now Ignacio had a strange feeling inside him. It was like when you look at someone you know but cannot remember that person's name. He felt deeply that answering that question could lead him to a destination he already knew but had forgotten how to get to. He checked his initial aggressive reaction and replied:

"Of course I'm happy! I'm a successful businessman. Naturally I have economic problems, like everyone else does, but I'm making progress. I have everything I want: my house in Lima and another one at the beach, my cars, a good wife and two children. I've achieved a great deal, and I have prestige in business circles." Ignacio felt that he was answering the question with all his artillery and that the enemy was now on the ground. By speaking of his possessions, he had built great impenetrable walls around himself with all his achievements.

The master replied: "I did not ask you what you have achieved or what your possessions are. I simply asked you whether you feel happy."

The master's response had penetrated the walls as easily as the sea destroys a sand castle. Ignacio was disarmed. At first he was tempted to persist rationally with his point of view, but something unusual was happening to him; he felt something like an intuition, an intuition far more powerful than anything he could express with ideas. He didn't know why, but he had the feeling that standing before that man was like recognizing himself. Then he began to see quite clearly a profound truth: he might deceive other people, but faced with that man's question about his happiness, he could not tell a lie. It was a fact that if he were a happy man, he would not have needed to look for help in a spiritual guide. Just then the worst thing that could possibly happen occurred: a tear started rolling down from the corner of one eye. He was overcome by a feeling he was powerless to control. He was being vulnerable before the aggressor, and yet he still considered himself the stronger of the two. A few minutes and many tears later, Ignacio finally replied:

"No. I don't feel happy."

Then the master spoke as if he had known Ignacio's reply in advance:

"There was once a peasant who had a well-loved horse. One day the horse fell into a deep pit. He tried to get the horse out, every way possible, but the hole was too deep. After days of vain attempts, the peasant decided to kill the horse, to put it out of its misery. He began to throw earth into the pit to bury the horse and suffocate it. But as the man threw the earth in, the horse shook it off its body, refusing to die, and lay on top of the earth. Little by little the pit was getting filled with earth, and the horse managed to stay on top of it. Finally the horse was high enough to jump out of the hole."

Ignacio listened to the master with interest. But he didn't understand what the story had to do with him.

"The energy you transmit to me is the energy of fear, anguish, rage, and unhappiness," continued the master. "I feel in you much suffering and loneliness. You are most probably going through a difficult time, like the horse in the story. You can respond to these difficulties by letting yourself be buried by your problems, worries, and difficulties. Or, like the horse, you can make use of them and take them as an opportunity to free yourself and achieve happiness. If you have come this far, it is because you have the intuition that this is the road and that I can guide you."

While the master spoke, Ignacio began to feel a very strange sensation of closeness. It was as if he had known this man all his life. His discomfort had turned into a feeling of confidence and warmth. The master, with the fire of his love, had melted the iron armor and the coldness surrounding him.

This was the first time in many years that Ignacio had allowed himself to show his vulnerability. He had always kept his emotions hidden. He considered that showing them was a characteristic of weak persons. Life had taught him that the only way to achieve success and avoid being used was by being tough and insensitive. Ignacio had hidden all his emotions in an interior safe-deposit box and had lost the combination many years ago. Now that the master was opening it, the emotions were flowing out desperately like doves set free from prolonged captivity. He felt as if he had met a friend he loved, a friend he had not seen for a long time: himself.

Nevertheless, his rational side came out, too. While he was sitting in the master's room, his inner ear buzzed with messages like "This is absurd!" or "What on earth are you doing, Ignacio? React!" But for some reason that he did not understand, the charisma of the master calmed him and made him feel that he was in the right place.

"I don't understand, Master," Ignacio stammered, with a broken voice. "I'm supposed to be happy. I have all that I need to be happy, but the truth is—"

"Ignacio, you cannot buy happiness. And happiness cannot come from the logical or mathematical process of adding up your achievements, your goods, your relationships, or your position in society. Happiness is felt, not thought. You have tried to be happy rationally; like wanting to enjoy the harmony of a tune just by reading the musical notes on the score, or to smell the aroma of a perfume by reading its chemical formula. The one who feels is not your mind but your spirit, and you have left your spirit aside for a long time."

Ignacio told the master about the difficult situation he was going through in the office, and he also spoke about his heart problems. He told him that the doctor had recommended meditation as a form of relaxation.

"Your stress and anxiety are merely symptoms of a greater problem," explained the master. "Dealing with the symptoms helps, but it does not solve the problem completely. It is like having a tank with a lot of little holes through which the water leaks and floods the floor. We can spend time sponging the water up from the floor, the symptoms, but the floor will continue to get flooded. The other possibility is to deal with the real problem by filling in the holes in the tank. Ignacio, you also have a tank of happiness, but it has many holes and your happiness leaks out from all sides. You have to learn not only to stop the leaks but also to create happiness in your life."

"But tell me, what do I have to do?" asked Ignacio, now beginning to think that the master really could help him.

The master regarded him in silence for a few seconds and then started to look for something among his things. His hands moved as if following some kind of undecipherable melody, an internal, slow rhythm which gave the impression that every movement had been deeply studied. Ignacio, hardly aware of it himself, was watching and growing calmer by the moment. The master picked up a small wooden chest that contained some crumpled pieces of newspaper. He carefully selected one of the pieces of paper and took a seed from it.

"In this chest I keep seven seeds of happiness. Each one of them has within it a profound lesson that will help you back onto the right road. We will start with this one."

The master gave Ignacio the seed. He held it carefully, as if it were a newborn baby. He felt that his whole life now depended on it.

"Go and plant this seed. Come back when it starts growing and I will help you to decipher its teaching," concluded the master.

Ignacio went home, greeted his wife and his children who were playing in the sitting room, walked through to the garden without anyone seeing him, and planted the seed. However, he decided that before believing everything the master had told him word for word, he would look up some information about meditation, and this would either boost his willingness to go ahead with it, or, on the contrary, confirm his suspicions. He took a long time on the Internet. He grew more and more astonished as he read how seriously the matter was taken. Among many other things, he found studies that showed that the persons who practice meditation reduce their oxygen consumption, reduce the secretion of stress-generating hormones, and increase their immune system. He discovered that in 1989 a magazine had published a study that analyzed senior citizens introduced to meditation. The study reported that in a short time these individuals showed significant and positive changes and finally lived longer than the control group of seniors who did not meditate. He also found an article about a Doctor Dean Ornish, who demonstrated that forty patients with heart problems had been able to reduce the plaque of fatty deposits that was blocking their arteries by means of meditation, yoga, and a strict diet.[3] After two hours, Ignacio had printed up a file of data and studies that convinced him that meditation was indeed very important for health.

⸎

From then on, every day after work the first thing he did was to look at the place where he had planted the seed. He hoped to see a little magic plant that would miraculously solve all his problems. But nothing grew. Then he watered it carefully, trying to give it the exact amount of water it needed to grow. His wife, who had been watching him for several days, said:

"Ignacio, what's happening to you? In all the years I've known you, I've never seen you water the garden before."

Ignacio had decided not to tell anyone about the master. All his life he had laughed at his wife and any friends who believed in spiritual or esoteric things, and he was not about to give them the pleasure of finding out his secret.

"What's happening, Honey, is that the doctor told me that the best relaxation therapy is gardening. You know . . . you're in contact with nature and you give your mind a rest. I've bought some seeds to plant them to make the garden look better."

His wife was satisfied with the explanation, and Ignacio now had an alibi to prevent anybody from asking questions about his gardening activities.

---

[3] J. Stein, "Just Say Om," *Time,* August 4, 2003, p. 48.

CHAPTER TWO

Watering the First Seed

Ignacio had been watering the seed every day for four weeks, but that little spot in his garden looked the same as ever. Nothing had grown there. Highly frustrated, he felt around in the earth and took the seed out: it was exactly the same as the day he had planted it.

"What's gone wrong? I've treated it like gold, but it hasn't grown," he said to himself, and started to have doubts: perhaps all this stuff with the master was pure foolishness and he was wasting his time. What message of wisdom could a plant contain? Or perhaps the seed wasn't growing in his garden because he didn't have the right to find happiness. . . . His wife had told him that plants perceive human energy and perhaps his kind of energy was preventing it from growing. Anyway, it didn't matter so much why it wasn't growing; the point was that he had not been successful at growing it. Ignacio felt useless and foolish, and he didn't like that feeling. He was frustrated and bitter with himself. He decided to go back to the master to get an explanation.

He arrived at the house like a soul possessed, knocked insistently at the door, and didn't even notice the garden when he was taken in to see the master almost at once.

"Master!" he said, seething with impatience. "You're making me waste my time! I've invested four weeks watering this stupid seed and nothing has happened! What is the message of wisdom that I'm supposed to discover? That businessmen are bad gardeners? If anyone in the office finds out that I've been watering a magic seed, they're going to think I'm the world's biggest idiot. Let's stop playing games. Teach me your relaxation techniques, which is what I've really come for."

The master looked him deep in the eyes and calmly told him:

"I gave you a seed that had been crushed by a hammer. It will never grow."

"Then why the hell did you give me the stupid seed? To make a fool of me? Is that what this is all about? In order to be happy we have to be humiliated and feel useless?"

"Ignacio," the master said, "children are like seeds. We have an enormous potential when we are born, like a tree of life capable of reaching the greatest heights. But if our parents crush the seed, that is, if they mistreat us, humiliate us, constrain us, and do not value us or give us affection, the seed will not grow. Or if it does, it will produce a weak, limited tree. I wanted you to experience for yourself how impossible it is to make the seed grow, so that you will never forget this idea. However, unlike seeds, human beings who have been crushed as children are able to grow, develop, and be happy. But to do so, they need to know themselves, to become aware of their past and understand how it affects them in the present. The first seed of happiness is self-knowledge."

Ignacio was listening to the master with a strange mixture of fascination and skepticism. His eyes went from the face of the master to his quiet hands, and from there to the walls with all those pictures of men who had doubtless already walked the vast roads of education of the spirit. Suddenly, Ignacio felt very small before that ancestral wisdom. Again he had managed to raise his aggressive state of mind to a state of peace and tranquility. The master had showed that besides possessing great wisdom, he was truly able to make a student learn the lesson.

After a pause, the master continued:

"When we are born we come into the world with the amygdala, the part of the brain that registers emotional memory, already fully developed. On the other hand, the cortex, the part in charge of conscious rational memory, gets built up little by little. Therefore, if a child goes through difficult times that produce strong emotions, these emotions are recorded in the emotional memory but not in the rational memory. In other words, the sensations derived from difficult times in childhood are recorded in an emotional memory we are not aware of. Technically, this memory is called the "unconscious memory" and it has the peculiarity, unfortunately for us, of being atemporal; that is, we remember as if it were yesterday. We carry with us for life a whole set of strong emotions that we are not conscious of."

Ignacio was losing the thread of the master's words.

"But Master, what does all this have to do with the seed?"

"When our parents crush us while we are only a seed, we have our unconscious memory full of destructive emotions.

Because of the nature of the brain, we carry these emotions with us all our life. The worst of it all is that they manifest themselves in our present, but we are not aware of this. Destructive emotions sabotage our interpersonal relationships, our security, and our sense of personal value, and they often prevent us from achieving happiness."

"But if the destructive emotions of my childhood are in my unconscious and I can't remember them, how on earth am I ever going to be free of them and be happy?" asked Ignacio.

"When people go to the movies they are so absorbed with the movie that they forget it is only a screen with an image projected on it," continued the master, with the self-confident assurance of a doctor prescribing an infallible remedy. "They forget that they are living a fantasy, and they suffer, cry, and are filled with joy at what they see as if it were real. But if a person goes to that movie theater and looks in through a side window, that person will see the situation as it really is. He will see a group of people watching a film that is not real, but also he will see that these people act and feel as if it were so."

Ignacio listened attentively as if each word contained the key to a riddle.

"It's the same in everyday life," continued the master. "We project our unconscious memories onto the screen of the situations and people in the present. It may be in the office or at home with your family, wherever, but your unconscious memories come to the surface and interfere in your life. I am like the person outside the movie theater. As you tell me about the problems, situations, and difficulties in your past, it will be easy for me to observe the projection of your unconscious memory on the screen of your life. As we decipher your unconscious projections, we will start exploring episodes from your childhood that can give us clues about your conduct. In this process you will get to know yourself better and you will understand why you act in certain ways that do not make you happy. Ignacio, the human mind is like an iceberg. The conscious mind is the tip that is outside the water. But that iceberg has an immense mass of information submerged under the water that we cannot see: the unconscious. The more consciousness and knowledge you take from your unconscious, the more freedom you will have and greater your capacity to be happy will grow."

"How do you mean?" asked Ignacio.

"For example, let us imagine a person who was treated badly during his childhood, and whenever he made a mistake he was shouted at and punished violently. If this person is asked to meet a goal that he finds difficult to achieve, he will start to have a destructive internal dialogue. He will feel useless, foolish, and unhappy. He will be angry with himself; he will feel that it is all his own fault. He will project onto the present situation the same feelings that he experienced in his childhood. Does that sound familiar?"

"But surely it's normal to feel terrible and guilty when we make mistakes?" interrupted Ignacio, who was gradually getting the feeling that his soul was a transparent window to the eyes of the master.

"You feel that it is normal because you have lived like that all your life," replied the master. "A nearsighted person who does not use glasses perceives reality as something blurred, and he thinks it is normal until he buys glasses. When we make a mistake, or when things do not work out as we had wished, we have no reason to feel useless or foolish or guilty. We should understand our error, learn from our mistake, and seek other alternatives without detracting from our self-esteem. The sensation of feeling useless is most likely a projection of some episode from your childhood; when you made a mistake then, someone probably made you feel that way.

"But it would be wrong to think that problems like these only happen to people who were mistreated in their childhood," continued the master. "Children whose parents allowed them boundless freedom, in the mistaken belief that they were bringing them up better that way, can also develop unconscious traumas. Childhood is like climbing a mountain, with your parents as mountain guides. As I said before, if your parents mistreat you in their attempt to take care of you, pushing you roughly against the mountain wall, you create traumas and pain in your unconscious mind. But if your parents leave you completely alone and let you go too close to the edge of the precipice, you will also develop phobias and insecurities that will become lodged in your subconscious. Children need to feel that their parents set up barriers so that that they will not fall over the edge, and these barriers are the limits."

Seeing that Ignacio was beginning to understand, the master concluded, "When you drink a cup of tea made from a tea bag, the water in your cup is gradually tinted a darker color. In the same way, in different situations in life, when our childhood has been difficult, we are like tea bags. We color the situations with dark emotions put away for a long time in our mind, but unfortunately we are not aware of that."

The master finally asked Ignacio to return the following day to start the process of self-knowledge.

⁓

While Ignacio was driving home, he reflected on his relationship with the master. A strange phenomenon was taking place. When he was there with the master, he felt that the master was transmitting great wisdom to him. His comments appeared sensible and logical to Ignacio. But the farther away Ignacio got, the more absurd the whole affair started to seem. How could our experience as children affect our lives so much? What was all this about a unconscious memory influencing our conduct? What did his childhood have to do with his feeling foolish or useless? Nevertheless, something inside him told him he should continue exploring that path.

Besides these references to childhood, emotional matters were another topic that Ignacio was uncomfortable talking about. He thought that everything he had achieved in his life had been possible thanks to his mind and his ability to block out and control his emotions; the only thing emotions had brought into his life was problems. He regarded emotional people as weak, incapable, and vulnerable.

Ignacio reached his house in San Isidro and went up to his study on the second floor. This was his favorite place, a kind of hiding place from the world where he could be alone to think or work. It was really a large library, with fine mahogany bookcases from floor to ceiling, full of books that were mostly about management and business. His desk was an elegant piece of furniture, imported from England. He had the latest model of computer with every possible accessory attached. Everything was impeccable and very tidy. This was Ignacio's throne. Here he felt he had power and control. He usually went to his throne room only when he felt threatened. Ignacio had learned a strategy to remove feelings of weakness and vulnerability. He would simply isolate himself at his desk to work on his office things, surf the Internet, or read the latest book on management. Today was one of those days when he needed to escape from the world. He felt distressed and he didn't know why. Within a few minutes, Ignacio was concentrating on the costs of a line of products he was thinking of importing. He had, once more, managed to hide and drown his emotions. Everything was under control.

Things were not getting any better in the office, but although the work continued to pile up and there was no end to conflicts, he had promised to visit the master the next day at six o'clock. On one hand he wanted to go and explore a world that was new to him, but on the other hand he felt that it was all a waste of time, especially now that there was so much work to be done. Forcing himself, and with many doubts, he got into his BMW and drove to the master's house.

When he arrived, he had to wait an eternal five minutes before the master could see him. This used up all his patience.

"Look here, Master," Ignacio said with authority in his voice, "the truth is that this whole subject of self-knowledge seems interesting to me, but I wouldn't like to waste time discussing my emotions."

Ignacio described to the master his strategy of burying himself in his work in order to control his emotions, and he showed his pride at being a person with full control over his psyche.

"The winners in life are those who manage themselves with their mind, not with their heart. I'm perfectly clear about that," affirmed Ignacio.

The master, who was listening to him calmly, excused himself for a moment. A few minutes later he came back with a glass of water, which had some ice in it.

"Take this glass and try to sink the ice with one push," said the master, handing him the glass. "Do it so that the ice stays sunk as long as possible."

Ignacio couldn't take any more.

"Master, I'm tired of you not listening to me and then going off on a tangent with your ridiculous games. I'm telling you about something that is important to me, and you want me to sink this piece of ice."

"Trust me, Ignacio, everything in life has meaning. Push the ice down."

Ignacio pushed the ice down, with resignation, feeling rather ridiculous. The ice sank in the water for a few seconds, but then it rose to the surface again. He did it again, and once more the ice came back to the surface.

"What are you trying to teach me now?" asked Ignacio ironically. "That I am the piece of ice because I don't have emotions? And in this state I'll never be able to enter into wisdom which is the water? Let me tell you something: the only way to survive in this ocean of problems I live in is to be a block of ice and not show my emotions. As you've seen with the ice, it's the only way to come up time and time again."

"An interesting interpretation, Ignacio, but that is not the meaning I wanted to illustrate." The master took a deep breath and looked into Ignacio's eyes. "When we have childhood traumas, as I explained before, the emotions from these episodes float to the surface. If you drown these emotions and block them out, which is what you have told me that you do, it is like pushing the ice down. But as you have seen, the ice always comes up again. Unlike the ice, which you can see floating back to the top, our blocked-out emotions come to the surface, but we do not see them, that is, we are not aware that this is happening. The only way to make sure that these emotions do not come back is to dissolve them, like the ice in water. This can be done with patience, and raising the temperature of the water. Ignacio, you must raise your emotional temperature and become integrated again as a person. You cannot go through life imagining that you are a robot, because that is simply self-deception. You must understand that you have an emotional aspect and a rational one, and it is necessary to integrate the two in order to be happy."

Seeing that Ignacio did not quite understand, he continued: "If a person comes to you to tell you something very sad and you do not want to hear that person, you can put your hand over his mouth. But he will still communicate his sadness to you with his expression and his tears; that, you cannot prevent. Ignacio, inside you there is a very sad person who speaks with painful emotions and you are covering his mouth in order not to hear him; you are hiding that person and drowning him inside yourself. But remember that that person cries too, and each tear surfaces in you and influences your conduct without your realizing it."

Once again, the master had managed to disarm Ignacio's rationality. Ignacio had attacked him as a disciple of judo attacks his master. But the master had dodged the blows and used the force of his assailant to put him into a vulnerable position. What

Ignacio did not know at the time was that this position would allow him to start growing.

"Right," said Ignacio. "You win. What must I do?"

"Tell me, Ignacio, how was it at work today?"

"The truth is . . . terrible," said Ignacio, indignantly. "When you have incompetent people working with you, everything goes wrong. Look, today a client called me to complain that we were three weeks behind sending him goods that he had already paid for. He said we were unprofessional and he was thinking of going over to the competition."

"Tell me, Ignacio, what did you feel while you were listening to him?" asked the master.

"I was furious and desperate. I felt helpless, stupid, and incapable. I went to the head of deliveries and shouted at him that he was incompetent and inept. I warned him that if he made one more mistake, I'd fire him. I did that in front of all his people so that they'd learn to do quality work."

"Do you not think, Ignacio, that your reaction was very aggressive?"

"It seems normal to me," replied Ignacio. "I've reacted like that all my life. My father taught us kids that you have to pay for your mistakes."

"Tell me more about this, about your father. Can you give me an example?"

"Let's see." Ignacio closed his eyes, as if searching far back in his life. "I remember that my father was always very strict with us. He wanted us to be well dressed all the time, my brother and me, and we always had to do what he wanted. If we disobeyed, we had to pay the consequences. One Sunday afternoon, when I was four and my brother Hernán was five, my father had ordered us to put our best clothes on because someone was coming to visit. We got bored waiting, so we went out to the park in front of our house. I remember that I slipped and fell and I was covered in mud from head to toe. We knew that if father saw me, he would give us a good beating. My brother tried to clean the mud off me, but it was impossible. Resigned, we went home to face the fireworks, but we never imagined it would be so awful. My father saw me and started to shout and insult me with words I didn't understand but that sounded horrible. I remember his face, so full of hate and rage. He grabbed me by the arm and took me to the shower. He opened the cold water and put me under it. While he washed me with the freezing cold water, with my clothes still on, he kept on shouting and started hitting me. I hadn't opened my mouth, I hadn't even cried. I was receiving the punishment with dignity and I did not intend to cry. He was hitting me hard, but the worst was the slaps on my face. When the physical torture was over, the worst was still to come, his shouts: 'Who do you think you are? What kind of fool are you, to get all filthy like that! Tell me, who are you? Idiot, answer me!' I said the words that were in my heart: 'Daddy, I'm a boy.' When I said those words, tears came into my eyes, but I was able to blink them back and I didn't cry. My father was always saying that boys don't cry. I knew that if I cried he might start hitting me again."

The master followed his words attentively, and seeing that Ignacio seemed to be getting a great weight off his mind, he gestured to him to continue:

"Go on, tell me more."

"I remember once when it was my brother who was punished. I was six years old, and Hernán seven. A friend invited him to his house one Sunday. My father told Hernán that he would pick him up at six o'clock. When it was time, my father asked me to go with him to pick Hernán up in the car. But Hernán was not there at his friend's house; he had left an hour earlier. My father got back in the car, worried, and started looking for him all over the neighborhood. While he looked for him, he cursed Hernán: 'That little idiot, who does he think he is to disobey me! What kind of fool leaves without letting me know!' I didn't move and I didn't say a word. I didn't want to give him a chance to transfer his anger onto me. I was paralyzed. After an hour of searching, we went home. My brother was already there—he had walked home. My father grabbed him by one of his feet and lifted him up. He held him up by his foot, his head dangling near the floor. He started kicking him in the back and shouting at him for disobeying. Then he went straight to the bathroom, and holding him by his two feet, put his head in the toilet and flushed it. While my brother was choking with the toilet water, my father carried on insulting him. I couldn't move, I was so terrified."

"That is a terrible scene. And what was your mother doing?" asked the master.

"My mother never interfered with anything my father did or said. He was the man in the house and he had to be obeyed. Although my mother didn't go out to work, we had very little contact with her. She was not affectionate; she was rather cold and impersonal. The most important thing for her was that everything should be tidy. She spent all day buying clothes, fine ornaments, and expensive appliances for the house. She was either out shopping or having tea with her friends, but she was never with us. She was only interested in herself."

"Now I understand why you shouted like that at the head of deliveries," said the master.

"What is it that you understand?"

"In the first place, that violence is *normal* for you because you grew up with it. This is why, if someone makes a mistake in your office, you do exactly what your father did with you when you made a mistake. What is worse, you relive your past, inverting the roles: you assume the aggressive, domineering role of your father, and you give the person you are mistreating the role of the frightened child. Also, it is probable that you actually go around looking for people's mistakes in order to relive episodes of aggression experienced in your childhood. You feel close to the memory of your father when you assume the aggressive role."

Ignacio experienced a strange mixture of admiration and amazement.

"Do you think that could be true?" he asked incredulously.

"It is difficult for you to realize," replied the master. "Remember that you project your unconscious emotions on to the screen of the individuals and situations around you. If you want to see what you are projecting and you are too near the screen, you will find it difficult to see properly. Like at the movies: when you are sitting near the front, you do not see well, but if you sit farther back you can see the picture perfectly well. That is how it is for me. I am farther away from the screen of your life; you, on the contrary, are right up close. I can see what is happening clearly; you see it blurred."

The master observed that Ignacio's facial muscles were relaxing. This showed that he was understanding.

"It is clear now why you are so frightened of showing your emotions," continued the master. "You are really scared to death that your father, who no longer lives physically but who is very much alive in your own mind, will mistreat you and humiliate you. You still keep in your mind your father's message: 'To be a man you must not feel and you must not cry.' To complicate things, you reinforced this message with your mother's coldness and her distant attitude. What is more, because of the way your father treated you, since childhood you have been carrying around with you these sensations of fear, distress, rage, help- lessness, humiliation, and ridicule. As I told you before, these unconscious memories are not forgotten; they remain present until they can be understood and digested by you. These are the emotions that you do not want to feel because they bring you too much pain, isn't that so?"

Ignacio was destroyed. He felt distressed. Once again, he struggled to hold back tears. The words of the master had melted the rational ice that blocked out his inner conduct. Now he began to feel how the emotions were flowing through his body. He felt much pain and sadness, he felt sorry for himself, and he felt rage against his parents. As he remembered his past and associated it with his present, he began to discover that the pieces of the jigsaw puzzle that were jumbled up inside him were beginning to fit together. He began to feel human.

"Ignacio," continued the master, "do not be afraid to feel, do not block your emotions. Let them out."

There were a few moments of silence. Then the master continued:

"There is a story about a peasant whose field had recently been sown. He heard a loud noise on his land. When he ran to see what was happening, he found something very strange: a jet of black liquid was coming up from the soil. He was worried that this substance might spoil his crops, so he called his family to help him cover the hole. The pressure was so strong that all the family members had to hold a plank down on top of the hole to prevent the substance from coming up. They stayed there for several days, without leaving to eat or sleep, but after a week, they could not resist any longer. So they decided to let go of the plank, and a great black fountain jetted up. But after a few minutes, this jet turned into clean, clear water, which the peasant and his family quickly channeled into a reservoir. Finally, the water helped them to grow because they were able to extend the area of their cultivated land."

Seeing that Ignacio was frowning as if he was trying to understand something but couldn't quite grasp it, the master explained:

"Ignacio, what is happening to you is the same as what happened to that peasant. You are so frightened of the black waters of your emotions that you block them out. I want you to know that everything you keep back, stays back there. Everything you cling to enslaves you. Ignacio, let the black waters of your emotions come out and you will see that afterward clear waters will start coming, which you will be able to channel in order to develop your life."

"What must I do to get rid of all the black waters I have inside me?" asked Ignacio in distress.

"First of all, you must not block them or keep them in. Do not be frightened to let them come out. When you feel anguish, pain, or fear, feel the emotions. They are a part of yourself. Do not bury yourself in your books or your work. What you need is to integrate your rational nature with your emotional nature."

The master paused to make sure he was being understood. Then he went on:

"Second, try to look at the screen of your life from a distance, so that you see the situations as they really are. When you feel hatred, rage, or indignation, observe your emotions and ask yourself whether these are not your unconscious feelings coming to the surface. Ignacio, in your life you are walking in a dark room and you keep tripping. Your room will continue to be dark; it cannot be made light quickly. But what you can do is to light your way with a match, to see what you have tripped over. When you act aggressively or you treat someone in the office badly, switch on your inner light and think about your behavior. Analyze what emotions and thoughts led you to act in that way and relate them to some episode in your childhood. As you start feeling your unconscious emotions and you understand them, linking them with your past, the ice will start dissolving and they will not come back again."

"But sometimes it's necessary to deal with subordinates drastically," argued Ignacio. "You don't have the slightest idea—"

The master raised his hand, as if trying to erase Ignacio's sentences, and he continued:

"Remember that when you react aggressively in the office, the only loser is you. With your reactions you do not induce the person who made a mistake to improve or to think about his actions. All you achieve is that this person will comment all around the office how neurotic you are. He sees your reaction as being so exaggerated that he will not take your comments into account. What you want is for your people to improve their work and be more efficient. What your mental father wants is to punish and mistreat the person who made a mistake."

Ignacio left the master's house and got into his car. He felt totally distressed, choked with emotions that were pouring out. His life was like a soda bottle full of emotions that he had tried to keep the cap on, but now the master had shaken it vigorously and opened it. He felt a flood of emotions that overflowed and invaded his whole being. It was strange, he was alone and yet he felt accompanied by someone very close to him, like his best friend: once more he had that sensation of finding himself. It was his emotional self, which had been buried for a long time.

When he got home, he slipped into his study and poured himself a whisky on the rocks. For a few seconds he was tempted to bury himself in office work and forget the world, but he didn't. He started playing with the ice in his glass and remembered the master's words. Then he began to review other bitter episodes from his childhood. He stayed there for hours, feeling the emotions that sprang up like fireworks. What a paradox: he was happy to be feeling unhappy! Really, he was happy to be feeling human again. He thought about how he treated his children and his wife. There were many similarities with the way he had been treated as a child, and he thought that this could be a never-ending chain. His father had been mistreated and then his father mistreated him. He was also mistreating his children and this would make his children mistreat his grandchildren later. And the worst of all was that this all happened unconsciously. He had to break this chain. His children were four and three years old, and he was in time to change. He did not want to crush the seed of his own children and make them live the hell that he was living.

◦◦◦

The next day he felt better; in his sleep he had managed to mitigate his emotions. He arrived at the office and people brought different problems to him that made him forget the episode with the master completely. Ignacio was working again as if nothing had happened.

Toward the end of the afternoon, Gustavo, the finance manager, came into his office. He closed the door and, referring to the marketing manager, he said:

"I'm sick and tired of that fool Pedro! He's always messing things up. He wants me to pass unbudgeted expenses, he hires salespeople and doesn't let me know. The other day it looked like fraud; he had three salespeople who were not on the payroll and he wanted me to pay them. He doesn't get his reports to me on time, he doesn't follow procedures. Do you know that we had five thousand Christmas cards printed for our clients and can you believe that he mailed out only four hundred? Ignacio, we've thrown away about two thousand dollars! Can you believe it?"

Ignacio was irritated. How could Pedro be dumb enough to throw away the company's money when it was going through such a difficult time? He stood up immediately and before Gustavo could say anything else, he pressed the intercom.

"Pedro, come to the office right now!" he shouted.

When Pedro entered, he saw Ignacio at his desk looking furious and Gustavo looking scared.

"Listen!" Ignacio rapped out coldly. "I'm tired of your sloppy work. It's losing money for the company! How much longer do we have to put up with your mediocrity?"

"What are you talking about?" asked Pedro, surprised.

"I'm talking about the ridiculous number of cards you had printed up for Christmas! Do you think we're swimming in money? What are we going to do with the four-thousand-odd cards that never got mailed? Charge them to you?"

Pedro felt that he was the victim of a misunderstanding. He tried to explain:

"But there's not a single card left over."

"Gustavo said you ordered five thousand and mailed only four hundred cards to our clients."

Gustavo, who was witnessing this scene, had never imagined that Ignacio was going to react like that, putting him face to face with Pedro. He wanted the earth to open and swallow him whole. Pedro looked at Gustavo indignantly, and expressed his disapproval with a gesture.

"What Gustavo doesn't know," he said, "is that we gave the other forty-six hundred cards to our sales force for them to hand to our clients personally as part of our campaign to give better service."

Ignacio had been inflating the balloon of conflict by attacking Pedro for his alleged mistakes. But Pedro, with these last words, had pricked it with a pin. There was no longer any need for conflict. The cards had been delivered, and in the best possible way. Ignacio looked at Gustavo. With a disapproving gesture, he said:

"Next time you want me to make a fool of myself, let me know in advance."

At that moment a picture of the master came into his mind and he remembered his words about tripping in the dark. He realized that he had tripped again. He had shouted at Pedro and attacked him unfairly; he had behaved like a neurotic person, and was only just becoming aware of it. He realized it, but the damage was already done, and he was unable to turn the clock back.

He apologized to Pedro for the misunderstanding, but Pedro was hurt. Ignacio did not know how he had gotten himself into that problem. There were so many problems with the competition, he didn't understand why he was wasting his energy on internal rivalries. He looked at his watch. It was time to visit the master. He left the office, got into his car, and set off.

At the master's house, Ignacio, disappointed with himself, described the incident.

"Master, I didn't realize. You don't know how stupid I feel," concluded Ignacio.

Nothing seemed to come as a surprise to the master.

"It is not easy," said the master. "You must be patient. You cannot change so many years of habits from one day to the next. This is a long process. Remember that you have been driving an automatic vehicle and you did things without thinking. Now you have to drive a car with mechanical transmission, and you have to be more alert to know which gear to use. Believe me, the fact that you have realized your mistake is a big step forward."

He paused so that Ignacio would feel more comfortable, and continued:

"Tell me, what do you believe you did wrong in this situation?"

"I was definitely wrong," started Ignacio without hesitating, "to shout for Pedro to come into my office and attack him for something that wasn't true. I should have made sure of the information before I spoke to him."

"I agree," said the master. "That was an error, but it wasn't the first one. The first mistake you made was to let Gustavo speak badly to you about Pedro behind his back. If you want to create an atmosphere of trust in your organization, do you not think that encouraging gossip goes against that goal? Next time someone wants to tell you something negative about another person, ask him if he has already spoken about it directly to that person, and above all, listen to both parties. And very important, you have to set the example. You must be very careful not to speak about people behind their backs. Remember that subordinates learn from what the leader does, not from what he says."

He paused again to give Ignacio time to think. Then he went on:

"Now tell me: what did you feel when you had the two managers confronting each other?" asked the master.

Ignacio thought for a while as he searched for the words to express what he had felt at that moment.

"To be quite honest, I felt a kind of pleasure. I felt that it was right, that there should be a winner and a loser. I suppose I wanted to see blood flow. I wanted the weakest to lose."

"As we saw last time," continued the master, "you look for violence in order to evoke your father. Do you remember any incident in your childhood that might be associated with this?"

An image came into Ignacio's mind of one of his most unpleasant experiences:

"Now that I think about it, yes. My father loved to make me fight with my brother. He used to tell us that we should practice at home so that we would be ready to beat up anyone at school. But he didn't want us to pretend to fight; he wanted us to really do it, without gloves, with our bare hands. I remember that he used to take us to the garage and make us fight there. If we didn't, he would hit us. He loved to cheer us on during the fight, shouting at us and manipulating us from outside. He used to tell me, 'Fight, stupid! Are you a girl or a fag?' I remember that once my brother hit me on the nose and it started bleeding. I wanted to stop fighting, but my father wouldn't let me. He said that men fought to the death, whether they were wounded or not."

"Do you realize, Ignacio, why you are so keen to see blood?" asked the master. "As a child you learned that this was the way you should behave. In this case, in your mind, you were your father motivating the fight, and Pedro and Gustavo were you and your brother as children."

"But what can I do if I had such a violent father and all this is stored in my unconscious? How on earth am I to free myself from this?"

"For the moment, there is no other way than little by little becoming aware of your unconscious emotions, reviewing how they manifest themselves in your present life. As you understand them, they will slowly lose their influence on you. When one has to walk blindfolded along a path where there are several bonfires, one can avoid the fires by detecting their heat. That is what you have to do, Ignacio, in real life. When you have emotional fires that lead you to act aggressively, even if you can't see them, at least detect their warmth and control yourself. The more aware you become of your patterns of conduct, the greater will be your capacity to improve."

While he slowly stood up and turned to one side, the master continued:

"Now you are ready to receive the second seed." He went to the chest, took out one of the twists of paper, opened it, picked up the seed with great care, and handed it to Ignacio. "Sow this seed, and when the plant begins to grow, come back so that I can explain its message of wisdom to you."

"But, Master, you're not doing the same as last time, are you, when you had me trying to make a crushed seed grow for a whole month?"

"No, Ignacio, this seed will grow into a plant. Come back here as soon as it comes up. Meanwhile, try to be aware of your episodes of aggressive conduct, your thoughts, and your destructive emotions."

CHAPTER THREE

The Sensitive Seed

Ignacio had been watering the seed for a month. He had taken care to water it every day, and this time it did grow into a tiny plant with little green leaves. All this time he had tried to be very much aware of his emotions, especially in his contacts with other people. However, he had not been very successful at controlling his aggressive conduct. He *was* learning to realize when he had made a mistake, but not until after the event. This he found frustrating. He knew now that he had a problem with aggression, but it happened when he was not conscious of it and could not avoid it.

That day, Ignacio was feeling enthusiastic when he got to work. He was missing his conversations with the master, and that evening he would be having his first appointment with him in a whole month. But his positive mood did not last long. He had a call from his local bank representative. His application for refinancing had been rejected because of the poor quality of the documents submitted: the cash flows were plagued with errors, the totals did not tally with the columns of figures, and the cash balances were wrong. The bank representative told him that the credit manager had said that if his client didn't even know how to do cash flows, how could the bank possibly lend him money?

As he listened to all this, Ignacio was steadily turning into a pressure cooker and the pressure was rising with the heat of his emotions. His company desperately needed credibility with the banks, and it was inconceivable that because of the incompetence of his finance manager, Gustavo, that credibility was being destroyed. He hung up the phone and strode to Gustavo's office. He was overflowing with a combination of fury, indignation, and impotence. All he wanted was to see his stupid finance manager face to face. Why were they all so useless? Why was he the only person who could do things properly? Ignacio burst into Gustavo's office; he was on the phone. Without waiting for him to hang up, Ignacio asked him:

"Did you review the cash flow documents before you sent them to the bank?"

Gustavo, seeing Ignacio's wild expression, hung up quickly.

"Of course," he replied. "I always review all my documents. What's the problem?"

"Look here, Gustavo," said Ignacio, "you are so hopeless that you don't even know when you have problems. I want you to know that you are an incapable professional; not only do you fuck everything up, but you don't have the foggiest idea that you are fucking it up! They called me from the bank to tell me that they've rejected our application for refinancing because we're incapable of doing a cash flow."

Gustavo began to experience that mixture of fright and distress that he recognized well. He did not understand what had happened. He had reviewed the document before sending it, and it was correct.

"That can't be so," he replied weakly. "That document was perfect."

Those words were fuel to the fire of Ignacio's hate and fury. It was like throwing a gallon of gasoline onto a bonfire.

"Don't be such an imbecile!" insisted Ignacio, his indignation fully aroused. "Why don't you admit it when you've messed everything up. Admit that you are incompetent, and you're a useless . . . "

Before he could finish the sentence, something happened. Ignacio abruptly put the brakes on his diatribe, like a driver who suddenly sees a child crossing the street in front of him. He began to hear echoes from the past: "You're a useless idiot!" "You're a useless idiot!" That was what his father used to shout at him when he made a mistake. He became aware that he was doing to Gustavo exactly what his father had done to him. Once more, he was unconsciously attacking someone.

The real Ignacio had just waked up from a dream. Sleeping, he had been driving the vehicle that was his body; waking up, he realized that he was crashing into his manager. This was the first time that Ignacio had been able to wake up and realize what he was doing while he was doing it. It was time to take the steering wheel and apologize.

"Sorry, Gustavo," he said quietly. "I'm sorry, I flew off the handle. The thing is, I'm so scared of bankrupting the company and disgracing my father's name that I get uptight all too easily."

Gustavo could not understand what had happened. It had never happened before. He had been ready to continue bearing the brunt of Ignacio's aggression, as he always did. In fact, he had already imagined himself out of a job! But a miracle was taking place: Ignacio was apologizing to him.

"Don't worry, Ignacio, we're all used to it. We know you don't have much patience. But don't worry, I'll talk with the bank and fix the problem."

Ignacio was beginning to understand how the mind worked. It was like a TV set. If someone sits down to watch a channel and someone else secretly connects a video and runs it, the prank will be practically impossible to spot. The screen seems to be showing a particular channel, but it is really a pre-recorded video. The human mind is the same. We tune in to the channel of real life, but automatically, and when we least expect it, a prerecorded video of our childhood is connected to our mental television. We are convinced that we are seeing real life, but it is a video of our childhood. This makes us distort every-thing and act neurotically.

Ignacio was calm now. He was sorry that he had attacked Gustavo, but at the same time he felt slightly elated because he had become aware of his behavior in time to apologize. Large drops of sweat rolled down his forehead, but he gradually glimpsed a thread of tranquility, a presentiment of inner peace that, although it had not yet arrived, was just around the corner. The day came to an end, and Ignacio drove to the master's house. He needed to talk with him.

∽◯∽

When he arrived, they showed him straight into the room where the master appeared to be waiting for him. Ignacio spilled out the whole story of the scene with Gustavo in the office. The master let him speak without interrupting him. His patient eyes bored into Ignacio's, and when Ignacio had finished, he started to speak, with long pauses.

"The lesson of the first seed was self-knowledge," he said. "You have seen the importance of understanding your past in order to understand how you react and act in your present. Now you are more aware of your neurotic behavior than you were some weeks ago. The experience with Gustavo proves this. However, I want you to know that this process takes time. The traumatic experiences of your childhood left pieces of firewood in your mind. This firewood flares up readily and creates fires and conflicts when any problem arises. In the measure that you understand, relive, and feel your childhood traumas, these pieces of firewood will become smaller and there will be no more fuel to make you explode."

Ignacio was impatient, like someone who has just discovered a tool and needs to use it.

"Master, now I understand how my mind works. But what can I do to become more aware, more in control, and not flare up so often? I need to change faster."

The master asked Ignacio to follow him into the garden. He gave him a piece of firewood and some matches for him to make a bonfire. Ignacio tried and tried to light the firewood, but it was impossible.

"This wood will never light, it's too damp!" he said impatiently, although he could already imagine what the master was getting at.

"I gave you a piece of damp wood on purpose," explained the master. "If your mental firewood is all damp, it won't light easily, and that will stop you from flaring up and reacting neurotically."

"Brilliant! But how can I make it damp?"

The master took Ignacio back to the room and sat on his cushion in the lotus flower position. His orange tunic fell in pleats that seemed to reinforce his air of calm and permanence. Then he continued speaking:

"You get your mental firewood damp by putting yourself in contact with your spirit."

"Spirits, no," interrupted Ignacio, "I don't believe in God or in spirits. Things are real, and all this about God is an invention of human beings, people who are frightened of the unknown and of death."

"Tell me, Ignacio, do you believe that a vital energy exists, something beyond this body we live with in this world?"

"Yes, I can accept that."

The master let a long minute go by. Then he continued:

"The message of the second seed reveals how you can make contact with your vital energy. How did you get on with the seed I gave you? Did you manage to identify any peculiarity in this plant?"

"Well, it's a plant that has very beautiful, delicate green leaves. But what does the plant have to do with my energy?"

"A lot," replied the master. "The plant you sowed is *Mimosa pudica*. It is called Sensitive Plant, and it has the peculiarity of closing up when it senses noises around it. When there is activity nearby, the plant hides in itself, it isolates itself and looks for inner peace. We human beings should do that at least once a day: leave aside activity and the outside and inner noise, and enter into contact with our inner energy."

Now Ignacio understood even less.

"And how do we do that?"

"Look, Ignacio, inside us there is an immense treasure of peace and tranquility. That treasure is our inner energy, but it is guarded by security guards: our thoughts. The only way to gain access to this treasure is by giving our security guards some time off. In other words, stop thinking."

"But it's impossible to stop thinking," said Ignacio. "What's the use of having a mind if we don't think? If I didn't think, where would my company be right now?"

The master was still sitting in exactly the same position, as if to symbolize the fixed idea that his words reflected.

"I do not say that it is easy," he continued. "People are not used to doing it. But if people could stop thinking for a few minutes every day, the world would be completely different. There would be fewer conflicts and people would be much happier. The idea is not to become an irrational being but to give your mind a rest. In the daytime you cannot see the stars; the brightness of the sun prevents it. But even if you do not see the stars, you know that they are always there. It is the same with the human being. The brightness of our thoughts prevents us from seeing our wonderful inner universe. But although we cannot see it, believe me, it is there, inside us."

"What inner universe do you mean?" asked Ignacio.

"Inside is your spirit, your soul. But if you like, call it your vital energy. When you manage to get into contact with it, many things happen. First, you feel peace and an incredible happiness. Something like when you meet up with a friend you have not seen for twenty years. When you meet him you feel a sensation of joy and happiness. Second, by having regular contact with your vital energy, you start recovering your innate qualities. You become a quieter person, more joyful, more loving, kinder, and desirous of serving and helping others. In the third place, and going back to the analogy of the firewood, you soak your mental firewood so much that after some practice it no longer catches fire. That is, even though you have problems and complex difficulties, you no longer generate uncontrollable rage, and you no longer flare up at work. Look, Ignacio. Human beings are like light bulbs painted black on the outside. When we stop thinking for a few minutes every day, we gradually scrape the black paint off. Our inner light starts to shine in our life, and we feel more joyful, but above all we tend to light up other lives."

Ignacio was following the master's explanation, but he still had some questions.

"How come not thinking can produce that effect?"

"When a turbulent river is full of mud, the only way we can drink water from that river is to let it be still in a pond for a few days. As it rests, the heavy sediments drop to the bottom of the pond and we can drink the clean water on the top. It is the same with the mind. When we withdraw from activity and stop thinking, our negative traits drop and what rises to the surface is the wonderful essence we have within, our best energy."

"But if we all have this inside us, why isn't it easy to see it?"

"Human beings are like old silver jugs: they have not been polished for a long time, so they have become tarnished. We are all used to seeing them dark and we do not know that that is not their real appearance. When we stop thinking, it is as if we were polishing them a little bit each day. There comes a time when the silver starts shining brightly. But if we stop polishing, if we do not practice every day, it becomes tarnished again."

"This technique of not thinking, is that what meditation is?"

"That's right," replied the master. "In the East it is called *meditation,* and in the West *silencing of thoughts* or *contemplation.* It is a technique that has also been used by the mystical movements of the Catholic and Jewish faiths. As you have said, it is not easy to stop thinking. Close your eyes and try not to think for a minute."

Ignacio closed his eyes and concentrated. When a minute was up, the master said:

"The minute is over. Did you manage to stop thinking?"

"Impossible," replied Ignacio. "I've never had so many thoughts in my life. You have no idea how many thoughts went through my mind. This is impossible!"

The master was silent again, and for a little more than a minute he seemed to take refuge in his own breathing. Then he spoke:

"So you must help your mind to do it. When people want to give up smoking, they use a series of strategies to reduce their habit. They use nicotine patches, they chew chewing gum, suck candies. . . . In this way their body starts reducing its need to consume nicotine and it is possible for them to get rid of the habit. It is the same with thought. It is a lifelong habit and it is not easy to stop doing it. We need a technique that will help us gradually.

"There is a story about a young man who found a wonderful lamp; he rubbed it, and a genie came out and offered to give him anything he wished for. However, he set a condition: that if the young man ever stopped making wishes, the genie would kill him. The young man asked for houses, carriages, jewels, but after a time he no longer knew what to wish for, and he was terrified that the genie would kill him. Then it occurred to him to wish for a pole. Once he had the pole, he asked the genie to climb up the pole and down again until he told him to stop. In this way the young man freed himself from the threat of the genie and was able to enjoy his life."

The master saw Ignacio's expression of concentration. He continued:

"In this story, Ignacio, the genie is the human mind. This genie has us threatened with thought unless we make him go up and down a pole like in the story. That is, we have to make him repeat a single thought several times. That is the first technique I want to teach you. You are going to choose a word that evokes a positive, agreeable sensation. For example, the word *peace*. You can choose whichever word you like best. Then, in silence, sitting on a chair or on a cushion on the ground, with your back straight, you will repeat it mentally for fifteen minutes. That is to say, we will get your mind going up and down a pole, and it will not be all that easy for it to go anywhere else. Thinking of one single thought is the first step toward managing not to think. Discipline your mind so that little by little it acquires greater concentration.

"However, it will not be easy. When you are repeating the word mentally, other thoughts will still come to you. That is normal, simply let them go and continue concentrating on your word. Little by little you will get into the habit and manage to have greater concentration. In order to learn to swim, children go into the water with floaters; but as they get used to the water and learn to kick, they start taking their floaters off. Repeating a word in your mind is a kind of floater. A learner needs it because otherwise he will sink into the depths of his thoughts. Later, with a lot of practice, you will be able to stop thinking without having to repeat any word."

Ignacio was ready to start. He chose the word *peace,* closed his eyes, and started to repeat it in silence. At first he found it very difficult. He repeated the word several times and then without realizing it he was already mentally in his office, at home, or solving some problem. Also, as never before, he became exquisitely aware of his own body. He felt small itches and irritations, changes of temperature in his skin, discomfort in his bones because of sitting in one position all the time. He let his thoughts go and continued trying to concentrate. Then, for a few seconds, after a time of concentration, he experienced something very strange, a slight sensation of love, like when his mother gave him affection when he was a child. He felt happy, but the sensation was very brief. His happiness was interrupted by the import contract for the Czech Republic that had to be signed the following week. Ignacio continued repeating the word, but he was unable to feel anything again. When he came back to himself, the master was observing him as if he were sleeping with his eyes open, in a position identical to his, but more perfect.

"Did you feel anything, Ignacio?" he asked, after a few seconds in which they both seemed to be coming back from somewhere.

Ignacio gave him the details of his experience.

"Just for a few seconds I felt something special. I really want to explore this technique more," he concluded.

The master continued:

"When a person is underground in a cave and cannot find the way out, he becomes discouraged and gives up trying. But if in his efforts to dig a way out he finds the tiniest ray of light, that will be enough to encourage him to continue digging and scraping until he can get out. Ignacio, you have just dug at the depths of your being and found a very little ray of light. Practice the technique every day in the morning and at night, and you will start having the same special sensation more frequently. The technique of repeating the word, as I mentioned before, will dampen the mental firewood that makes you catch fire emotionally and explode. But so that you will not explode, it is not enough to submerge that firewood in the morning and at night. I am going to show you a technique that you can use during the day, which will keep the firewood damp so that it will not catch fire. It is using your breathing."

"My breathing?" asked Ignacio, surprised.

"Yes. When you are threatened, frightened, and distressed, your respiratory rate rises. On the other hand, when you are rested, relaxed, or on the point of falling asleep, your respiratory rhythm drops and the breaths are longer. If you learn to be aware of your breathing and to keep it slow, you will dampen the firewood and you will not flare up. Also, breathing connects you with your energy. It is at this point that you will find the vital energy of the human being."

The master touched Ignacio's forehead at a point between his eyebrows.

"At this point," he continued, "a few centimeters into your skull, in the hypothalamus, is your essence. When you concentrate and visualize your breathing ascending to this point, you communicate with your vital energy. When you do that you will achieve greater peace and tranquility."

"How do you expect my breathing to go up to the hypo-thalamus, if it goes to the lungs? Do you want me to imagine it?"

"No, I want you to feel it. Your physical breathing goes to your lungs. What you have to learn to feel is the breathing of energy. With each breath you take, you take in air, but also *prana,* the energy that is in the atmosphere. This is the energy that you should raise toward the hypothalamus. This technique does not require you to close your eyes, just to divide your attention: half on the subject you are dealing with or problem you are solving and the other half on your breathing. In the office, when you have a difficult meeting or you are in the middle of an argument, concentrate in this way on your breathing and you will prevent yourself from flaring up."

The master paused, slowly gathered the edge of his tunic, and continued:

"Let's try it out. Leave your eyes open and concentrate on your breathing. Feel as if the energy of the air enters through your nose and rises to your hypothalamus. Feel the flow of energy with each breath. Leave all thoughts aside and just concentrate on your breathing."

Ignacio began to feel calmer and more relaxed as he breathed. When he breathed in, the air was colder and his sensation of peace and tranquility was greater. At first, it was difficult for him to feel the energy rising to his hypothala-mus, but then he got used to it. He was feeling a little sleepy, relaxed.

"What *is* this?" asked Ignacio when the concentration exercise was over. "I nearly fell asleep. What is there in the hypothalamus, a dose of Valium?"

The master smiled understandingly.

"A person who has to walk past a garbage dump to get where he is going holds a perfumed handkerchief over his nose; otherwise, he will have to put up with rotten smells. But if he does not use the handkerchief for some time, he will get used to the bad smells. It is the same with human beings. We live in a world rotten with anger, hatred, disputes, negativity, violence, anguish, and stress. But we do not realize that our mind, like our nose, has already got used to living this way. When you concentrate on your breathing reaching your hypothalamus, you are using the perfumed handkerchief we all have inside us. A handkerchief of peace, tranquility, calm, and harmony that is our spirit, our inner energy. This energy is the true essence of being. At first it will seem soporific to you, but then you will learn to enjoy its peace and happiness wide awake."

"How do you expect me to practice the technique in the office? If I have to concentrate on my breathing, how can I concentrate on my business?"

"When you are alone in your office, take a few minutes every two hours to concentrate on your breathing. This will give you the lucidity you need to prevent yourself from being carried away by your emotions. Then, when you are in a difficult meeting or receive a piece of bad news, immediately try to spend half of your awareness on your breathing. This will make you keep your distance from any stimulus and will stop you from exploding with negative emotions. If you are beside a person about to stab you but you take two steps back, the knife will not touch you. That is what the breathing technique does; it gives you the distance you need so that the office knives, that is, the bad news, conflicts, and problems, will not affect you."

The master took a ring off his finger and gave it to Ignacio.

"Ignacio, this ring has a mixture of gold, silver, and copper. When you use it you will be doing two things. First, you will protect yourself against the negative effect of the stars; and second, it will remind you to use the breathing technique in your life. Next time you feel threatened, touch your ring and immediately afterward concentrate on your breathing."

Ignacio left the master's house with a happy expectancy. He felt that he had received a treasure and that he should take care of it and keep it safe. Now he knew some magical techniques that would enable him to be calmer. But also, if he could master them, they would enable him to be a person superior to others, with the capacity to make better decisions, and with a high degree of self-control. It was incredible that no other businessmen knew about this. This was certainly an advantage for him. He had better not tell anyone; and he would practice it secretly so that nobody would suspect anything.

Ignacio got home and the first thing he did was to go into the garden and look at his plant. There was the little Sensitive Plant. Ignacio went up close to it, wondering what would happen, and mischievously gave a loud shout. The leaves immediately went limp and closed up, as if the plant had a spirit inside it that wanted to keep its peace and tranquility. The plant stayed like this for a few minutes, until it assumed that there would be no more loud noises. Then it expanded and showed its beauty again. The leaves looked more beautiful than before, as if the moment of introversion had recharged the plant's energy. What the master had said was true. The Sensitive Plant was living proof of the importance of finding an inner space away from the deafening noise of thought.

⟳

By the time another month had gone by since his last visit to the master, Ignacio had found his space for meditating without anyone noticing what he was doing. He locked himself in the bathroom in the mornings and at night, and spent ten to fifteen minutes repeating the word *peace*. He had felt that sense of peace again, but only a couple of times. The other times, the result was a feeling of relaxation—which was also helping him deal with the stress at work. Generally speaking, he felt calmer and more balanced, even though things in the office were not any better.

That day was very important for him. At midday he was to give a presentation on his company to a potential client who was very important because he could produce an increase in sales of more than 15 percent. The client was particularly demanding with regard to quality. Ignacio had prepared a presentation using all kinds of audiovisuals, such as video and computer photos. Someone from the office would be going to the client ahead of time to install the equipment. Ignacio went into his office early; he ran through his presentation, had his routine meetings, and at half past eleven he got ready to go to the client. He asked his secretary whether the person in charge of the audiovisuals was already in his place. The secretary called the client to confirm this, but the employee had not yet arrived. Ignacio had him searched for all over the office, and finally they found him fixing an assistant's computer.

"You idiot!" shouted Ignacio, very upset. "What are you doing here? You're supposed to be at the client's office!"

"Sorry, Boss, but I thought the meeting was later," replied the employee in a resigned tone of voice, clearly expecting to be tortured and thrown out of the company.

Ignacio wanted to kill him. How could people be so irresponsible? As he was getting ready to attack verbally with all his energy, he remembered the ring that the master had given him, and he remembered his words. While he touched the ring, he started to become aware of his breathing. He felt it rising to the hypothalamus for a few seconds; he paused while he concentrated on his breathing, and calm returned. Truly, that breathing dampened the mental firewood and stopped it from catching fire. Ignacio thought: "What do I have to gain by shouting at this person? Apart from giving him the excuse of saying that I'm crazy and I don't respect people, I'll just be wasting valuable time."

"Come on, then, I'll take you. Try and get everything set up as quickly as possible," Ignacio told him in a friendly tone of voice. "And next time be more careful."

The assistant, frightened, immediately got into the car with the computer. As they were leaving the parking lot, Ignacio asked him:

"Have you brought the video equipment?"

"Oh! No—did you need video equipment too?"

At that moment, Ignacio felt like hitting the assistant, but straight away he concentrated on his breathing and the impulse faded.

"Run and get the video equipment," said Ignacio.

While he was waiting, Ignacio concentrated on his breathing and was getting calmer by the minute. At times worrying thoughts came into his mind: he might arrive late for his appointment; the client, who was obsessive about quality, might be angry and then he would lose this sales opportunity. But then he would go back to his breathing again and calm down.

After a few minutes, the assistant hurried back to the car with the video equipment, and they set off. The assistant could not believe it. He was expecting to be thrown out of the company and out of work, but here he was traveling in the boss's car. He knew he had put his foot in it, but his boss had treated him with respect.

Ignacio, for his part, felt good at having controlled himself; he was full of peace and calm. He kept his appointment, and gave a magnificent presentation. He felt very sure of himself. He knew he was on the right track and this gave him a feeling of tranquility. This sensation of inner happiness meant that he was able to radiate a great deal of energy, conviction, and integrity during the presentation. He was thus able to persuade the client to work with him.

In the office, word went round about the incident. No one understood what was happening to the boss, but everyone agreed that he was changing. He was a better person, more tolerant and understanding. Ignacio now had reliable evidence that the master's techniques worked, and that having positive and peaceful thoughts was useful for business, too. Like a child who has been given a gold star at nursery school, he could hardly wait to tell his master about his success.

Once he was sitting on his usual cushion, Ignacio told him about the incident. He told him, also, that he had won the account of the client thanks to his good energy.

The master handed Ignacio a bucket full of white sand, but it was mixed with small black particles. Then he gave him a fairly large magnet, and said:

"Put the magnet into the bucket of sand."

Ignacio did so. The master began to explain:

"Look, just as the magnet attracted the black iron particles, your mind, if it is charged with negativity, will attract the negative consequences in the bucket of life. As a result, you will be surrounded by problems and difficulties. On the other hand, if your mental magnet is at peace, in harmony, with positive feelings and thoughts, in your life you will attract good things. That is what happened to you today. When you did not fly off the handle with your subordinate, by maintaining your peace and tranquility, you made your mind into a magnet for good and positive things. Another way of visualizing this idea is to imagine that we are all radio broadcasting stations and at the same time we all have a radio receiver. The music we broadcast on our station is our energy. When we are at peace and in harmony, we broadcast a wonderful tune. This reaches people's mental receivers without their being aware of it, but as they detect it they form a good attitude toward us. They feel the good vibration. It is like when you are looking for a radio station, you find a melodious song that you like, and you stop to listen to it with pleasure. When we are charged with negative energy, we transmit strident noises that scare most people away, except those who are accustomed to those noises or levels of negative energy."

"But how hard it is to be at peace in the office!" commented Ignacio. "I was lucky today, but I don't know if I'll be able to keep my cool tomorrow. The thing is that at work it's a perpetual war with the competition, with the banks, with the inefficiencies of the personnel, with the tough demands of the clients. . . . Everything conspires to make you tense, afraid, and anxious. I need to take my company to higher sales levels and profit levels to be able to live in peace and pay my debts. I won't be able to rest until I can do that."

"The thing is, Ignacio, that you are not clear about the true goal of business."

Suddenly it struck Ignacio as outrageous that the master, that patient gray-haired man in his orange tunic, should start talking about business. He might know a great deal about spiritual matters, but to give opinions on how to run a company was something quite different.

"What do you mean, I'm not clear?" Ignacio snapped. "I have been working twelve hours a day for more than twenty years. The objective of any business is to give an appropriate return to its investors, using strategies that will enable the company to maintain a competitive position, sustainable over time."

"What do you think is the objective of a train?"

"To take its passengers to their destination as fast as possible," replied Ignacio without hesitating.

"Typical reply of an executive in a hurry," said the master. "But why can it not be to take tourists slowly along its route to see and enjoy the landscape?"

"I imagine that that is also a valid objective. So the objective depends on the type of person."

"Right," agreed the master. "The majority of executives like you think that objective of the train of the company is to grow and reach its goals as soon as possible. They are desperate to make that train travel faster. Ignacio, we are tourists in this world, we live only eighty or ninety years, and then we go. The train of the company is an opportunity to develop ourselves and grow as individuals. The true objective of the company is to offer an environment that will allow you and your people to become fulfilled persons, to grow, learn, and develop. Profitability and money are means, not ends in themselves. Money is the fuel that enables the train to keep going. We have not come to this life to reach goals, Ignacio, or in the case of the train, to reach cities. We have come to learn and grow as spirits during the journey. We have come to remember that our real essence is peace and tranquility. From this point of view, if there are difficulties on the journey, or if the train has mechanical problems and stops, the passengers are not angry. On the contrary, they take the opportunity to get off the train, have new experiences, and learn more. That same attitude is the one you should have in the company. Take advantage of each difficulty, each crisis—the problems with the competition and with the banks, the interpersonal relationship problems—to make yourself a better person, to learn not to flare up in anger, to learn to serve and help, to teach and to give the best of yourself."

The master was silent for a few minutes, watching Ignacio. Then he continued:

"When a businessman, like you, once asked a rabbi why he lived so humbly, the rabbi answered him with a question: 'Tell me, when you go on a trip, where do you stay?' The man replied: 'I stay in small boarding houses.' 'And what are the rooms like in those boarding houses?' asked the rabbi. The man replied: 'Humble.' Then the rabbi asked him: 'Why do you stay in humble rooms?' The man replied: 'Because I am just passing through.' The rabbi took up his words and said, 'My good man, I am also just passing through this life. That is why I do not waste my time being entertained with material things and I prefer to live humbly.'

"Ignacio, in this life we are simply passengers in transit. When you leave your body and die on this plane, you will not take your goals with you, nor your achievements, your material goods, or your company. The only thing you will take with you is your spirit. Now it depends on you in what direction you focus your life: to accumulate these material things or to develop your spirit. The company is an excellent environment to make your spirit grow. You can learn to sail a yacht in a sea without waves and I am sure that you will easily master it. But where you really acquire the skill of navigation is in a sea with strong winds and big waves. The company is this rough sea, full of waves of change, of crises and problems. There you have the golden opportunity to learn and to develop your spirit."

Ignacio thought again of that recurring image of the surfer trying to advance against the waves, and no matter how hard he tries, he is lacking the skill and calmness to do it.

"That makes sense; yes, it's logical," he replied. "But I'm sure that I'll walk out that door and forget it. So many years I've been thinking and acting in a different way."

"I agree with you," affirmed the master. "When I explain these concepts to you rationally, it is as if I put a little water in your lake of knowledge. But the water evaporates quickly with the heat of the worries and obligations, and the lake dries up again. Nevertheless, underneath there flows an underground river full of the water of wisdom, which you must bring out. How? By meditating every day. Meditation puts you into contact with that river of wisdom, it brings the water to the surface and fills your lake. Your energy, your spirit, knows everything I am teaching you. You already have all the wisdom within you. Meditating brings it out little by little. It brings it to the surface and gives you an intuitive knowledge of everything I am teaching you. The time will come when you will no longer need me and my work will have come to an end."

"I've a long way to go yet," said Ignacio.

"Continue meditating, practicing your breathing, and remember all the time the true goal of business. Take advantage of every circumstance to grow."

Ignacio left the master's house in great confusion. He felt that all his life he had been running a race, trying to reach the finish line without realizing that the true goal was to develop and grow during the race. Deep inside him, he knew that the master's words made sense, but it was a radical change in his perception of life. How come everyone was mistaken? All businessmen and executives thought like he did. How come nobody had realized yet? Were they all blind or deceived by the system? Ignacio thought how society as a whole was oriented to the accumulation of material goods and to seeking happiness in meeting concrete goals; how advertising plays an important role in reinforcing the idea that by buying products people will be better and happier. "Perhaps the whole human race has been diverted from its real road and has not realized," he thought. He had one thing clear: the only way to discover it was by meditating. As the master said, meditation would bring to the surface a hidden knowledge that he already had inside him.

Two days later, Ignacio had the opportunity he had been looking for. All his family had gone to Ica for the weekend to visit his wife's parents. He had excused himself on the grounds that he had work to do, but really he wanted to stay at home alone to practice his exercises and do some deep meditation. Ignacio had been reading all kinds of spiritual and esoteric books, trying to acquire knowledge faster. He had been particularly impressed with one that talked of astral voyages and the possibility of leaving one's body. Ignacio was a rational person, but after reading so many books on the subject, he had doubts and at the same time hopes that this was possible. He had read that when you meditated deeply, it was easy to leave your body; you just had to want to do it.

He lay on the bed in his room and started by concentrating on his breathing for about thirty minutes, trying to avoid thoughts of any kind. He found it difficult for the first few minutes, but then he started concentrating better. He was relaxed, calm, and at peace; then he started to repeat the word *peace* silently. Again, thoughts came into his mind, but he continued to concentrate even more. After some minutes he began to feel something very strange, as if a sensation of love starting in his heart was rising up to his head. He began to feel great love and happiness; it was as if he were near people he loved a lot, like ecstasy, but very slight: more like a blessing. He felt drunk with love. At times he lost his concentration and the sensation went away. But when he was totally concentrated, it came back. It was as if the passing thoughts closed the door to that sensation of happiness he had inside. He continued concentrating on the word when he felt a strange sensation: that he was one with everything, that he was part of the walls of his room, the air, the bed, the garden. There was no separation, he was one with creation. All things were energy of love taking different forms, but they were all one. He maintained this lucidity for a few seconds, but then the feeling surprised him so much that thoughts crowded into his mind, and he lost it.

He stopped meditating and started reflecting on the experience. Could it be that what he had felt was what they call the *formless energy, The One?* Did The One really exist? He had felt something palpable, but perhaps it was his imagination or he was making it all up. It was a real feeling, he had felt the oneness with all based on love. Perhaps The One was a divine energy that was everywhere. It was not a question of faith; he had really felt something.

He meditated again and this time he found it easier to concentrate. In a few minutes he was feeling the sensation of love and peace. Again he experienced the sensation of being one with everything. He felt that he was pure energy, linked with everything around him. At that moment he remembered the books about astral voyages and he decided to leave his body. He said to himself: "I want to leave my body." But at the same moment the sensation of love went away and he lost the state of peace and tranquility.

Ignacio had read that the best time for leaving one's body was on getting up in the morning, just when one is half asleep and half awake. Since he was feeling quite sleepy and very relaxed, he decided to have a nap. Then perhaps he would be able to try leaving his body when he woke up. He really wanted to experience the sensation of being outside his body.

After a while, Ignacio woke up. He remembered that he wanted to leave his body and, half-awake, he told himself: "I want to leave my body." At that instant he felt a very strange sensation, a kind of lightness. He heard a very loud sound, like a deep vibration, and then he saw something that at first he did not understand. He saw the back part of a body, the head and the back, and he was watching. Then he realized that that body was his own, and that he was outside, watching it. He saw his body, but he could not move it; he tried in all sorts of ways, but he was no longer inside. He was terribly frightened and thought: "What if I can't get back into my body?" He tried to go back, but nothing happened, he had no control. He was panicking, desperate. He thought he would die, but then he found he was moving his hand and realized that he had reentered. He stood up, his heart racing. He walked around the room just for the pleasure of feeling his feet and his body. Then he sat on the bed, somewhat calmer.

"It works! It works! The spirit exists, I've felt it, I've been without my body, I can leave my body! There is life after death, we really are pure consciousness and we live in this body while it lasts." Ignacio set off to the master's house. He wanted to tell him about his extraordinary experience.

The master let him into his room. Ignacio sat on a cushion on the floor and told him everything, expecting sincere congratulations. Ignacio considered that leaving his body was a great step forward in spiritual development.

"Toys, Ignacio, you are just playing with the toys," the master declared.

Ignacio did not understand. He was suddenly disappointed and began to feel a mixture of bad humor and embarrassment.

"What do you mean, *toys*? I'm talking about an advanced spiritual experience. Didn't you hear me properly? Today I left my body!"

"Look, Ignacio, when you progress along the spiritual road of meditation, The One plays with you and gives you a series of toys. That is, he gives you extrasensory skills like mind reading, leaving your body, seeing auras, and looking into the future, among other things. . . . Most people who take up meditation are entertained with these toys. They spend time playing with all these extrasensory things and lose sight of the true reason for meditation, which is finding the divinity inside oneself. Meditation helps you to make contact with your true essence. It is like that pole-vaulter, who instead of training seriously for his jump, uses the pole to do pirouettes and acrobatics, to show off his skills to people. Undoubtedly, practicing pole-vaulting will not boost his sex appeal like showing off his acrobatics will, but it is the only thing that will take him where he wants to go. It is the same with spirituality. Meditation is not about sex appeal, making oneself attractive to other people: it is something we do by ourselves, not in front of other people. Progress is slow and the results are not spectacular in the short term, but it is the true road for the growth of the soul. Leaving your body, mind reading, and all those abilities may make you more popular, but they will not bring you nearer to your spirit. Today you have had the experience of leaving your body. Take the most important thing from it. The One has allowed you to confirm the existence of your spirit rationally and palpably. He has permitted you to clear up your doubts so that you can dedicate yourself to meditating more seriously. Take this opportunity."

Ignacio felt depressed. He had been looking forward so eagerly to telling the master about his achievements, and once again the master had deftly brought him down and was disarming him. The worst of it all was that everything he said made sense. He felt small, ignorant, and with much to learn.

The master, stroking his beard, spoke again in a dismissive tone:

"Now that you have learned not to dabble in phenomenology, I want to teach you a new technique. I consider it to be the most valuable one I can give you for meditation. I will give it to you on one condition: that you will not pass it on to anybody else. The other techniques you have learned, you may teach, but the new one, called Kriya Yoga, you may not transmit."

"But why the secrecy, Master? Aren't we supposed to help people to improve? Not that I want to teach the technique to anyone, but I'm curious to know why it has to be kept secret."

The master, as always, was expecting Ignacio's question.

"Kriya Yoga is an ancient meditation technique that has been handed down for centuries from master to disciple in India. It is a powerful technique and must be practiced correctly. Otherwise, it can have negative consequences. The only person who can teach Kriya is a disciple who, after many years of practice, has been authorized by his master."

"What is Kriya Yoga?" asked Ignacio, anxiously.

"Let's put it like this: if you want to go by car to a far-away city, hundreds of kilometers away, you have two options. Either you go in a small vehicle with few cylinders, and you take quite a time to get there, or you get into a powerful eight-cylinder vehicle and accelerate. Both cars are going to take you to your destination, but one will do so somewhat faster. Kriya Yoga is the eight-cylinder vehicle. It is a technique that will enable you to advance faster in meditation."

"What's it like?" asked Ignacio—full of doubts, but at the same time wanting to be given the centuries-old techniques to make quicker progress.

The master took a breath, crossed his legs, and stared into space.

"Look, Ignacio. The problem with the technique that I have already taught you is that when you try to concentrate, hundreds of thoughts crowd into your mind. Our minds generate three thoughts per second. It is difficult to break that habit but not impossible; you can eventually achieve that sensation of peace and love that meditation gives. You have advanced a lot using these techniques. The advantage of Kriya Yoga is that it teaches you a series of postures that, through certain physical movements, affect your nervous system and give you a better capacity for concentration. When you finally make your mind blank, you have greater facility for keeping it in that state for a longer time."

The master, patient and virtuous, started an initiation ceremony. Then he began instructing Ignacio in the techniques of Kriya Yoga. They practiced together so that Ignacio would be clear about each exercise. Ignacio ached a little, because the postures were demanding on the body, but on the third day he felt better.

The following week, the master handed him the third seed.

"Plant it," he said, "and come back when it is in bloom. Then we will talk about its teachings. Be patient, it will take a few months. Just concentrate on meditating every day and on being aware of your conduct as much as possible. Remember the true goal of life and business. Practice your meditation every day and add the Kriya Yoga techniques. You will make faster progress along this road."

CHAPTER FOUR

The Third Seed Grows

Four months after the last visit to the master, the seed had grown into a wonderful crimson rose tree, which led Ignacio to think that the teachings it contained were somehow connected with love. Every day, before going to bed and in the morning, Ignacio meditated for half an hour. He had taken it so seriously that this was a parenthesis of time that had to be respected. He applied all the techniques the master had taught him: repetition of the word, concentration on breathing, and the physical discipline of Kriya Yoga.

Since he had started practicing Kriya Yoga, Ignacio felt that his capacity for concentration had increased substantially. He could spend longer without thoughts and the sensation of well-being was greater. He clearly noted the effects on his mind. He no longer reacted explosively at work; he was more tolerant and aware of his conduct, but also he was more conscious of what other people were feeling. The meditation gave him a less ego-centric perspective on situations. Also, it enabled him to stand back from problems.

Another consequence of the meditation was that his charisma had increased. He was getting along much better in his interpersonal relationships and with his sales. In fact, he had become the best salesperson in his company. Before, he had never gone near the sales area. Now he went with the sales-people to the main clients, with very good results, because he felt more positive and more at peace with himself. He trans-mitted this peace to the clients and an instant bond of trust was created.

That afternoon Ignacio had an important appointment with a client. As was his custom, he went fully prepared and was successful in making the sale. He was almost ecstatic; he felt that he was a winner and superior to everyone. He was invincible. His company was better; sales had increased, and the company was paying its accounts in the banks. It had regained respect in the business world. He felt that he was now on a dif-ferent level as an entrepreneur.

With the intention of sharing his achievements with the personnel, he called all the important executives to his office to tell them about his success with the client.

"I want to tell you all that once again I managed to make the sale," said Ignacio euphorically. "Lately I've been taking charge of sales personally and the fact is that everyone can see the results. I by myself have increased sales by more than 30 per-cent. I am worth more than the company's ten salespersons put together. I wonder why everyone can't work like me—why is it that I can meet incredible goals and it's so difficult for you to do so? I need you all to work like me; I need everyone to be loyal to the company, to have faith in the company."

When they left, Ignacio did not know what had happened, but at least he realized that he had made some kind of mistake. He had perceived that the people were discontented, but he didn't know why. The company was better: why weren't they happy about it? He closed his office and drove to the master's house.

Again the large street door and the clean, pleasant façade. He felt that this place was his second home. It had gone from seeming like an oasis in the surrounding neighborhood to being a genuine spiritual oasis in which Ignacio refreshed himself after the daily conflicts.

Once he was in the master's room, he told him about the episode in the office.

"What did I do wrong?" he asked. "I wanted to motivate them, but it didn't work!"

"Tell me, Ignacio, did you plant the seed that I gave you?"

"Of course. I have a lovely rose tree with deep red flowers in my garden. I imagine that the message of wisdom must be something to do with love, right?"

The master had remained almost in profile until then, but now, before replying, he turned and looked at Ignacio with his penetrating eyes. He took a breath and explained:

"No. On the contrary, the message of wisdom has to do with the lack of love."

"But roses are a symbol of love! In all the Western world they are given as a token of affection and love."

"Yes, I know the customs. The rose is beautiful; when it opens its petals it displays a harmonious structure that seduces you, and it has a marvelous fragrance—but you can only admire it from afar. If you get too near, it will prick you. It is the same with people who are managed by ego. Like roses, they spend their life seeking admiration, prestige, status, and acceptance. But when you get near them, they end up pricking you with their egoism."

The master shifted his position, crossed his legs, and continued, half-closing his eyelids.

"The first seed I gave you was the seed of self-knowledge. It was important for you to start by knowing yourself, by becoming aware of how your past affected your present. You had to gain a greater awareness of your acts, thoughts, and emotions, and of the feelings of other people. Once you understood yourself more, you started to have greater control over your acts and decisions. But that was not sufficient. You needed practical tools to calm yourself down and resume a balance in your life. That was the second seed, the seed of meditation, represented by the Sensitive Plant. Meditation has enabled you to have more peace and quiet, maintain a state of positive thoughts, and above all keep your distance from problems. It has also continued to help you become more aware of yourself, of your true essence, and of what is important in life. The third seed, represented by the rose, is the control of the ego."

"But, Master, what *is* all this about the ego?" Ignacio interrupted.

"Ignacio, people like you, people who have had a difficult childhood, whose parents have mistreated them, have a wound in their self-esteem. Do you remember that the first seed I gave you could not grow because it had been crushed? If your parents hit you or mistreat you in your childhood, your self-esteem deteriorates. As a consequence, your mind creates an inferior personality that at all costs wants to conceal the fact that it does not feel competent or capable. That inferior personality is the ego. When we feel safe, we trust ourselves, and we feel that we have value. That is, if our self-esteem is high, we do not need to hide anything; in consequence, our ego is very small. On the other hand, when we feel insecure, fearful, frightened of life, we have an imperious need to hide this; in consequence our ego is big."

"But I don't understand what all that has to do with the rose."

"The point is, Ignacio, that the ego, in its eagerness to hide an inner reality that we do not want to see, develops a series of tricks behind our backs—well, behind our consciousness. For example, it is common for people who have low self-esteem to try to place themselves in situations in which they can feel admired, prestigious, and recognized. They do this because deep inside they feel that they are not valued; they feel insecure. It's like being addicted to a drug: they always need to be valued by those around them so they can feel that they are worth something. But if you draw close to these persons, you will see a thorny reality, a reality of fear and inner pain. Something like the rose, which wants to be admired but in reality if you draw close, you get pricked by its thorns. Today you have told me about an incident in your office. You called the people to a meeting to share the company's sales success, and you cannot understand why it did not work properly. The ego is the reply to your question. It was not you who organized the meeting, it was your ego. You sat everybody down and told them about all *your* achievements, not the achievements of the company. As if that were not enough, you told them 'I am worth more than ten salespeople from this company' and you asked them 'Why can't you work like me?'"

"But that's completely true! I *am* the only one who has been able to sell so much!" exclaimed Ignacio, indignant at the master's comment.

"I do not doubt that you are a good salesman, Ignacio, but you are also the owner of the company and you are much better qualified than all your personnel. It is evident that you should do better than your subordinates. But is it necessary for you to rub their noses in it? Or could it be that you repeat it to your people because you don't really believe it yourself?"

Ignacio stood up. He was furious.

"Of course I believe that I am competent! I tell them so that they will learn, so that they will sell more too, so that they will react and improve!"

He was blinded by his ego and the master could read in Ignacio's face, like an open book, each of the sentiments that tormented him. It was necessary to confront Ignacio with himself, even if it was painful. It was the only way. The master half closed his eyes again and breathed deeply, trying to transmit some of his calmness to the irritated Ignacio. Then he spoke:

"And how do you think that telling them that you are better than ten of them will make them react? Well, I think they *are* going to react, indeed, but not at all the way you want them to. Calm down, Ignacio, and realize how you are being manipulated by your ego. If your objective was for them to learn and react, it would have been better to teach them with humility some of your sales strategies."

Ignacio sat down. He felt very bad; he felt like crying, and the tears were not long welling up in his eyes. He felt pain in his chest. He had a sensation of abandonment and lack of affection. It was as if the whole episode had brought up unconscious memories from his childhood. Really, what he had wanted when he gathered his people in the office was to receive affection and love.

"Master, now I understand," said Ignacio brokenly. "My ego is the personality, the engine that directs my acts to seek the love I failed to receive as a child."

"Yes, Ignacio. What you are really seeking is love, understanding, and acceptance, but you manifest it through conduct that hinders interpersonal relationships."

He was silent again, and let his hands rest on his knees. Once more the room had become charged with the peace of the dialogue.

"When your bicycle has a flat tire, you can use a bicycle pump to blow it up by hand. But if the tire has a puncture in it, however hard you try, no matter if you work for hours on end, it will not inflate. It is the same with the ego: it makes us go through life with a flat tire that sabotages our relationships. All the time we have to be pumping this tire up—trying to get people to accept us, admire us, and recognize us. The problem is that this tire is punctured, and we will never be able to stop inflating it. We will end up being slaves to the bicycle pump, and we will carry it around with us, ready to use it at any moment."

As he understood better, Ignacio felt relieved of an enormous weight, as if a bag that he was carrying on his shoulders were dropping the stones inside it one by one. In their place was an empty space, open to curiosity:

"But apart from the mistake I made in the office, boasting about being the best and the most successful salesman, I'd like you to explain what other kinds of conduct the ego uses to express itself."

"Before going on to other kinds of conduct, let me give you another example in the same category. Do you remember that you came one day full of excitement to tell me that you had managed to leave your body? That is the problem with the esoteric aspects such as leaving your body, mind-reading, or reading the future. They enlist your ego. You feel that you are a chosen one; you believe you have a power that nobody else has. You feel that you have reached a high spiritual level. You want to show your abilities to everyone and tell everyone about them, in order to feel accepted and in demand.

"There again you are a slave of the bicycle pump. Most individuals who enter the world of meditation are captured by their ego and get stuck in the phenomenological aspects. As I said before, forget the phenomenology; it is not the important thing. Another behavior typical of the ego is to speak about people behind their backs. It is like the elevator mechanism: it is fixed by a pulley or a rope with a weight on the other end. For the elevator to rise, the weight has to descend. When you speak badly about people, what you are doing is throwing the weight onto them, that is to say, you put them down so that your own ego can rise. Whenever you comment that someone is incapable, incompetent, or lazy, what you are really saying is that you are not like that, and this makes you feel superior. This is also like the person trying to pump up the punctured tire. When you speak badly about someone, you pump yourself up, but then you become deflated again because you have an inner puncture, and what is commonly known as *backbiting* becomes a drug for you to use in order to rise again. The problem is that, just like a drug that gives gratification, it also produces a series of negative consequences. For example, you get full of bad vibrations and negativity. Speaking badly of people is harmful. You create an atmosphere of distrust and lack of motivation in the office."

"Yes," interrupted Ignacio. "In my office there's a lot of that. Everyone speaks badly of everyone else. Especially the human resources manager. That woman is a real backbiter. When she's with me she never speaks badly of anybody, but people have told me that when I leave the room she starts criticizing everybody."

"Ignacio, do you realize that you are backbiting a back-biter? You were careless for a few seconds and your ego took control of your mind again. It made you describe the errors of your manager so that you would feel superior."

"But, Master, if I can't judge, how can I interpret life? In my job I need to evaluate information, make decisions, judge situations and people's conduct. If someone works well I should judge him, evaluate him, and congratulate him. If someone works badly I must judge him and show him he has made a mistake so that he'll be able to improve."

"There is no problem in judging, Ignacio. The problem lies in the fact that your ego uses judging as a tool to inflate itself. Your ego is permanently at war, trying to inflate itself at all costs. Like a soldier, it has a uniform that enables it to camouflage itself. It camouflages itself by justifying its acts with sophisticated reasoning, like the reasons you just gave me. The only one who knows when your ego is manipulating you to judge, find mistakes, or criticize is yourself. You will have to be alert and very much aware to prevent your ego from manipulating you."

Seeing that Ignacio understood everything, the master paused to give him time to reflect. Then he continued:

"They say that a very critical woman saw from her window that new neighbors had moved into the house across the road. She looked at them and saw that they were very dirty. The next day she looked at them again, and said to herself: 'How terrible! How dirty these neighbors are! I bet they never take a shower.' She called all her friends to tell them about her extremely dirty neighbors, but she didn't find any of them at home. She was dying to tell somebody, when a friend came by to visit her. The woman didn't even greet her friend; she took her straight to the window and said: 'Look at these disgusting people, they haven't taken a shower in days, can you believe it?' The friend looked at the window and said to her: 'No, my friend, take a good look; it's your window that is dirty.' The friend wiped the window and then the neighbors looked perfectly clean.

"When people speak badly of others behind their backs, it is because their mental window is dirty. It is misted over with their ego, which tries at all costs to put others down in order to feel superior."

"But how can I change a conduct I have been practicing for more than thirty years? Besides, it is a very popular kind of conduct."

"A lot of people go through life as drivers of a train that always runs along the same rails. Their habits, the rails of the train, take them along predetermined routes and they never depart from them. You must grip the steering wheel of your life. Fill your tank of willpower and initiative and trace your own routes, those that take you to your real happiness."

Ignacio was astonished by the simplicity with which the master made him understand everything. He had to go as far as possible:

"Right. Backbiting, that is, looking for errors in people, is an example of the ego's tricks. But how else does the ego show itself?"

"Let me explain a couple more ways. The first, the killer conduct for teams, is singling out the guilty ones. When things are not going well in a team, the ego feels completely threatened. The worst thing that can happen to the ego is to be discovered, or for others to see that the person does not feel competent. Remember that the objective of the ego is to hide its inner failings, but above all, to hide them from you yourself. When we look for a person to blame, we cover up any possibility of showing ourselves up. The ego seeks to feel successful all the time, in order to hide the feeling of failure the person has inside."

"But isn't it important to identify who caused a problem? How will the person who made the mistake improve?" asked Ignacio.

"Ignacio, it is one thing to find who was responsible for a problem to help him improve so that it will not happen again, and it is quite another thing to look for the culprit to throw it in his face and put him down. Again I ask you: what is your objective? To raise your own ego or to get that person to improve?"

Ignacio nodded. The master continued:

"Another conduct typical of the ego is refusing to accept the ideas of other people. The ego wants to be seen as the best, the most intelligent, and the most capable. Since the person does not feel like that inside, he wants to reinforce it from the outside toward the inside. When the members of the team are intelligent and creative, they become a threat to the ego of the person with problems of self-esteem. In this situation, the ego becomes a killer of ideas. If someone proposes a brilliant idea that is accepted by the team, the person with the ego problem feels foolish. This person starts a destructive internal dialogue: 'Why didn't I think of that?' 'I am not clever,' or 'I am not creative.' He has a lot to lose, which is why he will try to discard other people's ideas. Imagine all the opportunities that are lost because of someone's internal problem."

Ignacio felt transparent before the eyes of the master and was becoming more and more embarrassed. That is why he gave in to the temptation to try and justify himself.

"But Master, I have all these ego behaviors that you have mentioned. What motivated me to make my company progress was my ego. I wanted to prove to the world that I was as capable as my father. I wanted to be successful and recognized and I've worked hard at it all these years. What could be wrong with that?"

"There is no doubt that the ego is an excellent economic and professional motivator. But is that your definition of success in life? Success in life is obtained when you reach happiness. You have lived by your motivation to meet goals, but you will agree with me that you have been a very unhappy person. Once again I ask you: what do we come to this world for? To meet goals or to be happy?"

"Both!" replied Ignacio with a mischievous smile. The master had become his friend.

"Correct, but let me phrase it this way: we come to be happy while we run the race to the goals. In that definition the ego is excluded. Remember that you will not take your goals, material goods, or prestige with you from this world when you die. You will take your spirit only."

"But what can I do to live without ego?" asked Ignacio.

"It is not easy to get rid of the ego. Few people in the whole world have managed to do so. But what you can do is keep it under control, reduce it, and be more aware of how it influences your conduct."

Seeing that Ignacio was about to bombard him with questions, the master held out his long hand to stop him; then he took a piece of newspaper, and lit it with a match. The paper burned up in a few seconds.

"Just as the fire burns and consumes paper, your inner fire should burn and consume your ego. I refer to the fire of your spirit. This you achieve by meditating. Every time you meditate, you burn a small portion of your ego. Little by little you will start reducing the efforts of your ego. You told me that you had discovered that the ego compensated the lack of love you felt inside. Well, when you meditate your inner flame of love comes up and fills your being with a sensation of plenitude and peace. You feel love from within. Then you will not need to cover your insufficiencies with external elements such as seeking approval, acceptance, or proving that you are the most intelligent. It is like a person walking through the desert, thirsty, with nothing to drink, and forgetting that on his back he has a tank full of water. He is so used to carrying the tank that he has not noticed that it is his salvation. We, too, have a tank of love inside us. We seek the water of love and acceptance outside, when we have it right here, inside us. Only through meditation will we obtain it."

The master stood up and started moving slowly around the room, the folds of his long tunic moving slightly as he walked. Ignacio noted that this was the first time he had seen the master walking around. He suddenly had the impression that this man did not need to talk in order to transmit wisdom. It was sufficient to observe each of his movements carefully to perceive that he belonged to a superior spiritual universe. After a few steps, the master continued:

"Coming back to the analogy of the ego and the punctured tire that we always have to inflate: meditation repairs the tire, or the ego, with patches of love that come from your spirit, so that you don't have to keep inflating it endlessly. There is another strategy to reduce the ego, but it is linked with the following seed."

The master took out the seed box, and gave Ignacio a twist of newspaper.

"Go and plant this new seed. Come back when you know what plant it is, to talk about its message. Try to be aware of your ego and control it. Do not fail to meditate every day. Practice the Kriya Yoga."

CHAPTER FIVE

The Message of the Fourth Seed

A month and a half had passed. The seed grew into a small plant with long, wavy green leaves. Ignacio's gardener told him it was a mango tree. Ignacio thought that the lesson of this seed must be associated with fruits or results. Unlike the other plants, this was a fruit tree. He was sure that the teaching had something to do with the idea of producing results in life.

Ignacio had lost all desire to practice phenomenological activities. He meditated half an hour each morning and half an hour at night, and he felt happy with this new habit in his life. But it was a different happiness from anything he had experienced before, permeated with calmness and love, and at the same time comforting and strengthening. He could not go to work or go to bed without meditating. His meditations were increasingly deep. The state of peace and tranquility gradually lasted more during the day. This enabled Ignacio to keep himself at a greater distance from daily problems. He flared up less and was much more tolerant with people.

He was also obsessed with trying to get rid of his ego. He had taken the advice of the master seriously and was acutely conscious of the ploys his ego used. Sometimes, before acting, he realized that his ego was manipulating him, and then he was able to avoid its unpleasant consequences. At other times he acted with his ego, but then he realized what was happening, thought about his conduct, and ended up being furious with himself. He wanted to win the battle against his ego, and he was determined to use all the weapons he had at his disposal.

That day he had the monthly meeting of the executive committee. They were to review compliance with the goals of the month and progress against the strategic plan. It was an excellent opportunity to manage his ego and prevent his ego from managing him. So far he had always started the executive meeting by assuming the leadership. But this time he decided to give each manager a turn to talk, so that they would all present their achievements and results. He would be a facilitator. The company was doing better, but in the past month its sales had dropped. This had created a somewhat tense situation in the management team.

Three managers—Alfonso, operations; Gustavo, finance; and Pedro, marketing—had finished their presentations, and now it was Roberto's turn. He was the sales manager.

"The truth is that we have not met our goals because of the economic crisis in the country. Things are tough and the clients are not buying. Besides, we had some problems with deliv—"

Before Roberto could complete the word "deliveries" Alfonso, the operations manager, started shouting, beside himself with anger:

"What delivery problem are you talking about? Don't be such a fag! Admit that it's your own fault you've failed, don't be spreading the blame around the whole company. It's your people who haven't sold anything!"

"If you had more control over your sales crew, we wouldn't be like we are now," added Gustavo, the finance manager. "There's no control! No reports! They all do whatever they like! How can we sell like that?"

Ignacio observed this dialogue with a feeling of rejection, and he could clearly see how his managers were being dominated by their respective egos. If this had happened to him a few months earlier, Ignacio would have jumped into the fray to destroy the weakest and make him pay for all his mistakes with his blood. But now he was fully aware of what was happening.

"Take it easy, boys," he interrupted. "We're not here to find culprits, we're here to help each other."

There was a sudden silence. All the managers were surprised by Ignacio's comment. Among other things, unconsciously, each one was thinking how Ignacio, the leader, would have reacted some months ago. He had them so used to dealing with problems by flying into a rage! The atmosphere remained tense.

"Remember that we are a team," continued Ignacio, "and in a team the idea is that although there are people responsible for the different areas, with clearly defined roles, we are all here to help the person responsible to meet his goals in any way we can. So let's think how we can help Roberto. Remember that all of us, sooner or later, will have problems too, and we're going to need someone to help us. So, please, without attacking anyone, let's try to say sincerely what we are thinking."

"But Roberto doesn't want to find solutions, he just wants to look for excuses and mess us all up in the process!" shouted Alfonso.

"Roberto, tell us, how can we help you meet your goals next month?" Ignacio asked him quietly.

Ignacio had managed to calm the atmosphere. His positive tone, quiet and peaceful, had spread to his managers. Roberto thought twice before opening his mouth:

"To tell the truth, the main problem I have is with *you,* Ignacio. For some months now you've been doing things in my area, you've been making sales yourself. Nobody doubts that you've had good results, but you have also taken away my people's motivation. They feel that you have stolen their best clients, and that way anyone can make good sales. And they feel that the only thing you want to do is to show off and rub in their faces what a wonderful salesman you are!"

The peaceful expression disappeared from Ignacio's face. He frowned, raised his voice and said:

"But what kind of an idiot are you! I'm trying to help you, and all you can do is attack me! Don't you realize that I am the only one who has saved this company from bankruptcy? If we had let your sales force sort out the problem, each one of you would now be at home living off your savings. Animals! Lazy, and on top of it, backbiters! You don't seem to have anything to do, because you all spend so much time criticizing other people."

The expression on the faces of Alfonso, Pedro, and Gustavo was one of acceptance of Ignacio's words, as if they were saying: "That's the Ignacio we know! We were starting to miss him." The sales manager felt intimidated and was unable to make a reply.

As soon as Ignacio stopped speaking, he realized that once more, his ego had taken control of his mind. In a matter of seconds, dozens of thoughts went through his head: *What an idiot I am! How could I have let my ego take control of me? I was telling them what not to do, and then I go and do it myself. What message am I giving my people? That I'm all hot air and I don't practice what I preach. I ought to apologize, excuse myself, tell them I was mistaken.*

"Well, let's leave it there; I'll have another meeting with Roberto to sort out the sales problem. Good afternoon."

Ignacio stayed on in his office, alone. He had not had the courage or the strength to tell them that he was mistaken, and that that was not the way to treat people. Why was it so difficult for him to accept mistakes? Why couldn't he control his ego? How easy it was to see people's egos! How easy it was to be aware of the emotions and reactions of others! But why was it so difficult to observe them in oneself and have self-control?

~ॐ~

With all these questions, he went to the master. It was incredible the way all his distress faded away as soon as he was let in through the door. For some time now he had gotten into the custom of stopping for a few minutes to look at the garden. At first this seemed strange to him, but then he became convinced that simply by looking at the quiet life of those plants, he could learn a great deal about his own life.

Sitting in the master's room, he described the whole episode of the executive committee meeting.

"Master, I can't manage my ego! Since you taught me that lesson, I have tried to make a big effort to keep it under control.

I made it my goal to beat my ego. But finally my ego takes the upper hand. I can easily see other people's egos, but I can't control my own. I try to, but when I'm least expecting it, when I have the most need of being aware, my ego takes control of me. What can I do?"

The master said, with a slight smile:

"Ignacio, I have the impression that your ego wants to get rid of your ego."

"Master, I don't understand. What *are* you talking about?"

"It seems to me that your ego is playing tricks on you. Now that you are determined to try and get it under control, it has disguised itself, and it is your ego itself that wants to eliminate your ego. It is as if your ego were a thief disguised as a policeman, pretending to look for the 'thief ego' to throw it into jail. He knows he can put it in jail, but in reality he himself has the key to the cell. In other words, you continue to be trapped."

Ignacio's expression showed how hopelessly confused he was.

"On setting yourself a goal with so much attachment and eagerness," continued the master, "and wanting to be the winner and beat your ego, you are acting with your ego. When you are angry, upset, or in a fury, you attract your ego. When you are at peace, with tranquility and balance, your ego retreats.

"The story goes that a master was with a disciple sowing seeds outside his temple, to embellish it with plants. Suddenly there was a strong gust of wind and it blew away almost half of the seeds. The disciple was angry, and he started complaining. When the master heard him, he told him: 'We have done the best we could. That is what matters.' A few days afterward there was a storm, and the rain flooded the temple and its surroundings. The disciple was furious. He felt that all his work had been wasted. But the master replied: 'We did the best we could.' Weeks later many little plants started coming up all around the temple. The disciple jumped for joy and the master told him: 'We did the best we could and that is what matters.'"

The master paused, placed his long hands on his knees, and continued: "The message of this story, Ignacio, is that one should always do the best one can and give the best of oneself, regardless of the results. Remember that goals provide you with direction, but the objective of life is to enjoy the path to those goals giving the best of yourself and keeping your inner peace and happiness. Ignacio, take things easy, be patient and tolerant with yourself. A habit cannot be changed from one day to the next. Do not set yourself the task of beating your ego. That is a trap that you must avoid. That implies that there is a winner and a loser, and it takes you indirectly to the ego. Set yourself the goal of walking with greater awareness along the paths of life and giving the best of yourself with each step. Do it with compassion and love for yourself. Little by little you will change. Meditation will help you in this process."

"Master, in the executive meeting I realized I had put my foot in it as soon as I stopped speaking, but I was unable to apologize. Why is it so difficult for me to accept that I am wrong and apologize?"

The master smiled again, like an understanding father.

"Remember that you had parents who mistreated you every time you made a mistake. For you mistakes mean very painful punishments, but above all they imply the withdrawal of affection on the part of your mental parents. At one level, in your unconscious, it is a terrible thing to make a mistake and that is why you try to avoid it at all costs. But, Ignacio, admit that you are much better than before."

"How can I be better if I make mistakes all the time?" replied Ignacio.

"Because now you realize that you make mistakes," replied the master. "The first step toward changing is to become aware. You now understand the mental processes; you recognize the emotions and actions of others. You recognize some of your negative behaviors and are able to manage them. With others you cannot do so yet, but you do have the ability to think about them afterward. When you first came to my house you had no idea of any of this."

"Thank you, Master, you are raising my ego!"

"No, Ignacio, it is a truth and a recognition that I give you with much love. But tell me, do you know what the seed was that I gave you?"

Ignacio smiled proudly:

"Yes, it's a mango tree. I imagine that the message has something to do with the fruits of life. We harvest what we sow. Is that it?"

"That's right," replied the master. "Each one harvests what he sows. But that is not the message. Let me explain it to you with a story:

"A rose was talking with a mango tree and it told the tree: 'In this garden I am the plant that gives the most to human beings. I give them my beauty and good looks. I give them a very rich fragrance. There is no one like me.' The mango tree said to the rose: 'What are you talking about? I let the humans come close to me; I protect them from the sun with my great shade. But also they throw stones at me all the time, but I don't mind and I give them my fruits with love. But if people approach *you,* you prick them maliciously.'

"Ignacio, the mango tree gives us the wise message of the importance of disinterested service. Our ego makes us act all the time in our self-interest: it wants to meet personal objectives that raise it, achieve goals, acquire status by purchasing expensive articles, solve problems. . . . Our ego puts glasses on us that are like mirrors, so that we are looking at ourselves all the time. Service is the opposite of ego. To offer disinterested service means going over and above the ego, taking off our mirror-glasses, and discovering how we can help other people."

Ignacio gradually understood the meaning of this new dimension: service. The master continued:

"A small wave asked a big wave for help approaching the beach. It said that it was very small and it wanted the big wave to give it a bit of its water. But the big wave refused to give it a single drop. The little one continued begging for help for a time, but the big one never relented. After a few minutes, both waves broke on the shore and merged in the sea. In the sea they realized that they were both a mere temporary illusion, and that all the water was a single unit: the ocean. It is the same with the human being. Each one feels like a different wave. The majority do not want to give up a single drop of their resources. But what they do not know is that afterward, when we leave this material plane, when we die, we will find that we are all one single ocean of divine energy. The form, intensity, speed, and size of each wave does not matter, we all belong to a single sea. But human beings concentrate on the differences and they do not see the unity. If your left hand receives a blow and is hurting, do you rub it and help it with your other hand?"

"Of course," replied Ignacio.

"You do so because you are convinced that it is your body. If we all understood that we are a single cosmic consciousness, we would help each other more."

Ignacio saw everything with a different clarity now.

"When I meditate," he explained, "sometimes I have felt, just for seconds, that I am part of everything, that the walls, the floor, the plants, and I are all one. Is that what you call cosmic consciousness?"

"Correct," replied the master. "When you meditate, you stop seeing the waves and you see the ocean. You feel like a particle of the whole divine creation. Meditation is gradually giving you a greater awareness of universal unity and it is helping you take off the mirror-glasses.

"There is a story that some people were once sailing in a boat, when one of them started to drill a hole underneath his seat. The other passengers shouted at him. 'What are you doing? Have you gone crazy?' The passenger replied: 'What's bothering you? It's my seat that I'm making a hole under.' And the others answered: 'The water will come up through your hole and it won't sink only you, it'll sink all of us.'

"It is the same with human beings. Each person concerns himself with his own things and does not realize that with his conduct he is sinking the whole of humankind. Ignacio, there is no greater happiness in the world than the happiness you feel when you help a third party. It is as if The One were rewarding you for aligning your actions with divinity. There are persons who have never meditated, but who have oriented their whole being to the service of others. These persons are very spiritual, happy, unattached, and have very little ego."

"But, Master, if a person gives disinterested service because he knows that it will give him happiness, doesn't that make it self-interest? Isn't is egoistic to want to have that happiness?" asked Ignacio.

"It is true that it is a selfish attitude to begin with. But what would humankind be like if everyone had that type of selfishness? That egoistic attitude then becomes blended into a sensation of giving and loving. Let us say that the self-interest of serving in order to obtain happiness is merely the wick of a great dynamite stick of love. The wick is used to detonate the explosive. But once the dynamite of service explodes inside you, you no longer do it out of self-interest but out of a vocation to serve that is born inside you."

"What I don't understand, Master, is why it is that if service gives so much happiness and love, so few people do it. People supposedly want to maximize their happiness; it would be logical for them to do it through service."

"The story goes that a person lost the key to a treasure chest and he was looking for it outside his house, under a lamp post. Since he couldn't find it, he asked for help. He even offered to share some of the treasure. Soon, a great many people were looking for the key. After two hours someone asked the owner of the treasure where he had lost the key. The owner answered: 'In my house over there. But I am looking for it here because there is no light in my house.'"

He paused when he saw that Ignacio had not quite understood, and explained:

"Human beings look for the key of happiness in the wrong place. Television is largely to blame. With its programs and advertising, television makes you look for the key of happiness in a place where you are never going to find it. Certain types of advertisements convince you that you will not be happy unless you buy a specific car or brand of clothes, or unless you use cosmetics or buy all kinds of appliances. You do not realize that most of the ads lead you to seek something that will benefit you alone. They have convinced human beings that happiness is achieved when they buy things or seek their own personal benefit. Precisely the opposite is true."

Although somewhat confused, Ignacio knew that the master was right.

"If I want to offer service, where do I start? Where should I help? In an old folks' home, an orphanage, a school for poor kids?"

"Start with yourself first, Ignacio. Service is an attitude to life. It means no longer thinking of yourself but rather thinking of others. You are giving a service when you listen with empathy to an employee who has a problem, and instead of throwing his mistake in his face, you help him to improve. When you are concerned for the growth and development of your personnel in the office, or of your wife and your children. When you simply give a thought of silent love to a person in the street. Your service can start at home, with your children, your family, and your business. The One has given you the great opportunity of being the owner of a business. In your business you can decide that the purpose is to make money and devote all your strength to this objective. Or you can decide that the purpose of your business is to be a means of serving society and a good environment for people to learn and find their happiness. In the second case, the money comes as a result. Another thing you can do is sell a share of your business to The One."

"I don't think that The One will want to buy my business. When I tried to sell it, nobody wanted to give me a cent for it," said Ignacio jokingly.

"Don't worry. The One has a special way of going into business. He would not pay you a cent for your shares either. But if you give him a small percentage of your earnings, he will reward you abundantly. In other words, if you donate some of your profit to charity organizations, that is, to The One, he will be your partner in the business. But be careful: The One is a good investor. He will make your business grow so that its profitability for charity will be increasingly high. Ignacio, all human beings have a *dharma* in this life. That is, a mission to fulfill, a lesson to learn in life. Ideally, the service you give will be aligned with your *dharma*."

Ignacio was feeling increasingly involved, and the strange feeling was growing in him that all his life so far had been like a game: it had kept him very busy, but there had not been much point to it.

"But how can I know what my mission is and what lesson I should learn?"

The master shifted very slowly, drawing his knees together on the cushion, and he placed the palms of his hands on his thighs.

"The lesson is easy, Ignacio. Try to identify the main difficulties in your life: there is the lesson that you have to learn. Remember: life on the material plane is like a university. If you enroll in a university, you will not start going to school to learn arithmetic. It would be too easy. You need to register in a course that offers you the difficulty necessary to stimulate your mind and motivate you to learn. It is the same with life on this plane. We come to learn a lesson in keeping with our level of spiritual development. If you want to know what your lesson is, just look at your difficulties, challenges, trials, and problems. Some of these problems have already become lessons learned that have made you grow and be a better person. Other difficulties, on the other hand, have marked your personality, leading you to destructive, negative behaviors. Those, precisely, are the behaviors you need to reverse. This is your test in life."

"Do you mean the difficulties in my childhood, for example?" asked Ignacio.

"Right. What was the result of your childhood? What characteristics did it create in your personality?"

Ignacio hesitated.

"Definitely impatience, intolerance, judging people negatively, and perhaps being negative in general."

"Well you have just discovered what you have to learn. Life has given you a difficult childhood precisely so that you will have the courage to grow, improve, and leave behind those destructive behaviors."

"Right, then, that is the lesson I have come to learn. But how can I identify my mission in life?"

"A spirit's mission is always oriented toward service. You can know what your mission is by observing the different circumstances you have gone through in life and discovering your real abilities and aptitudes as a person. In the first place, you are in the business world, you are an entrepreneur. Your mission must be related to that field. Another important aspect is that you are one of the few businessmen who practice meditation and are familiar with this philosophy. Perhaps your *dharma* is associated with communicating your knowledge and discoveries about this subject in the business world. Perhaps your mission in life is to sow the seed of personal improvement, meditation, ego control, and service among business executives and entrepreneurs. On one hand, you are a good communicator; you have passion and energy, which is what one needs most in order to communicate. I believe, Ignacio, that helping to awaken the executives and entrepreneurs by speaking to them about what truly matters in life is your *dharma*."

Ignacio had a shrewd idea where all this business of service was leading him, as it opened up before him like an unexplored field that he would have to venture into.

"But, Master, I have never given a presentation in public! That is definitely not one of my strengths. Anyway, I have always done my meditation in secret; even my wife doesn't know that I meditate. If I start speaking about this topic, I'll have all the executives in the city throwing tomatoes at me. Remember what I was like when I came. All I cared about was work, numbers, and achievement. The whole subject of spirituality seemed absurd to me. I'd never be able to speak about it in public."

The master opened his arms briefly and fixed his eyes on Ignacio's with a penetrating look.

"Ignacio, you asked me about your *dharma* and I have helped you to find it. Finally it depends on you alone whether or not you want to carry out your *dharma* in this life. It depends on you whether you want to use to the full the potential you have and the knowledge that you now master, or whether you want to let the opportunity slip. It is in your hands. There was once a great Jewish master called Zusha. He said: 'The day that I die and I am taken to the great celestial court, they will ask me: 'Zusha, why were you not like Abraham on Earth?' And I will say: 'Because I was not lucky enough to be born with his intelligence.' If they ask me: 'Zusha, why were you not like Moses?' I will answer: 'Because I was not born with his leadership skills.' But if they ask me: 'Zusha, why were you not like Zusha on Earth?' unfortunately I will have no answer for that.'"

The master's hands rested on his thighs again.

"Ignacio, do not be afraid to be Ignacio in this life. As for your fears, let me tell you that there is always a first time for everything. If you have never given a presentation in public, well, take this opportunity. Of course, prepare for it well, and put together a good one. You are a creative person, you will be able to do it.

"A dog once wanted to drink water, but every time it approached the lake it was frightened because it saw its own image reflected and thought it was seeing another dog. The dog was dying of thirst, but it could not get over its fear of entering the water and being attacked. A hunter saw the dog coming and going. He picked it up, took it past the shore, and set it down in the water. When the dog was in the lake, it saw that all its fears were unfounded, and it calmly started drinking.

"Ignacio, you are like the dog in this story. You are dying of thirst for service, but you are very frightened, too. Do I have to pick you up like the hunter and throw you into the water? As for your difficulties regarding speaking to businessmen about spiritual matters, success depends on how you do it. Prepare a rational presentation supporting your statements. Reach your public based on what they want to hear, but always putting your message across. I know you can do it. That is what you have come to this world for."

Ignacio knew that the master was right, but every time he imagined himself in front of an audience, he got butterflies in his stomach and his forehead was damp with perspiration.

"Master, I'm scared of talking in public. How can I lose that fear?"

"Very simple. Every time you give a presentation and you are standing in front of the public, think: 'How can I serve these people?' Since your message is going to help them to improve, and because you are going to give the best you have to these people, lovingly and disinterestedly, you will see that your fear will vanish. Fear comes to us because when we are in front of an audience, we feel that we are asking rather than serving. We are asking for approval, respect, and acceptance. Since we are afraid that the public will not give us these things, we are frightened. But if we go with the purpose of serving, with love and selflessness, the fear disappears."

Ignacio was disconcerted. He didn't know what to do. What the master was asking of him was an enormous challenge. But something inside him told him it was the right road to take. That he should do it. He felt as if he had a rock over his head, because of the tension he felt at the mere possibility of speaking in public on these topics. Ignacio was silent for a few seconds and then he said:

"All right, I'll do it. I'm not sure that I'll be able to do it well, but I'll trust your judgment on this, Master."

"Come back when you have given your first presentation."

౿☞

Ignacio had been coming home from work late every night for weeks now, grabbing a bite to eat, and heading up to his study to prepare his presentation. Two months after visiting the master, he had decided to speak about the four seeds that he knew: self-knowledge, meditation, ego control, and service. He thought he would focus on the business world and how these tools make it possible to form better teams, have greater productivity, and improve interpersonal relationships. He knew that he had to provide a great deal of rational backup—and not speak about spirits or The One because his hardheaded audience might think he was being pretentious or not take him seriously. The most difficult topic to address was meditation. Once more he went over the material he had taken from Internet months earlier, after his first interview with the master. He even spent some hours updating the information, and he noticed that the topic was always being renewed and added to with the results of the latest research.

Ignacio had discovered that the best time to work on his presentation was following meditation. Many ideas came to him, as if someone were helping him. It was as if the presentation had already taken place and he was merely remembering it.

In addition to using scientific studies from important universities, he wanted to prepare a highly professional presentation using computer graphics. The idea was to project an executive image while dealing with topics that were not usually thought of as executive ones. Ignacio wanted to give his presentation with plenty of audiovisual aids that he could hide behind. He thought that if he showed impressive pictures, people would look at the pictures rather than at him. He had also talked to a friend about his plans to give presentations, and the friend had said he could begin with his company. For Ignacio, these two months had been very special. It was the first time in his life that he was working for something that was not related to making money. It is true that he felt it was a challenge, and he knew it was for his own good. He was doing something to serve others, and that was completely new. He was delighted. He was preparing the presentation with a great deal of enthusiasm and sense of purpose, because he was doing what he really wanted to.

A date had been set for his first presentation. It was to be in two days' time, at seven in the evening. The friend had booked a hotel to take all his people so that they could listen comfortably. Ignacio had a strong desire to give the presentation; he had worked very hard, but at the same time he was very frightened.

He took two days off work and practiced his presentation out loud at least fifteen times. He wanted to learn it by heart so that he wouldn't have to read it.

At seven o'clock, he was at the hotel. He felt well prepared but at the same time very nervous and fearful. He had meditated for an hour before leaving home so that he would be fully in balance, but even so he was feeling anxious and distressed. All the time he concentrated on the fact that he was doing this as a service and that he would give the public the best he could offer, disinterestedly. This thought helped him reduce his tension for a while, but a few minutes later he would feel tense again. People from his office had arrived earlier and installed the projector for the computer images. Everything was ready and working. There were some two hundred people in the hotel conference room. His friend invited him to come to the speakers' table, while he went to the podium.

While his friend introduced him and described his background, Ignacio felt the threatening look of all those present. He felt flushed and his legs were trembling. His breathing rate had increased as if he had run a hundred-meter race. A drop of sweat slid down his face from the corner of his left eye. He made every effort to think about service, but it didn't work. The fact that his magic antidote did not work made him even more nervous. He thought to himself: "What on earth am I doing here? Why have you failed me, Master? The strategy of thinking about service was supposed to take away my fear, but it's not working!" Each second that passed made him more nervous. Finally, the worst moment came. His friend pronounced his death sentence: "And now I leave you with my friend Ignacio Rodríguez. A round of applause, please." The audience clapped loudly. This added to Ignacio's distress, because it committed him even more to giving a good performance.

Ignacio stood and went to the podium. He needed something to hold on to, for security. The podium was ideal because it also served as a barrier; it was like having a place to hide. At the podium, he looked at the people and felt that they were all bored. He had not yet started to speak and was already feeling like a loser. He felt that the people were thinking: "What are we going to learn from this idiot? He's a waste of time! He must be boring!" Each face he looked at confirmed his intuition that the people didn't want to be there. He thought: "I bet my friend made them come."

He signaled the person in charge of the projection to put the first picture on the screen. He needed to get the people to stop looking at him and look at the visual aids. But the boy at the computer, without meaning to, instead of pressing the forward key, switched the computer off. Ignacio saw how the picture faded and his presentation was lost. Everyone stared at Ignacio, waiting for him to say something, but he didn't know what to say. He was breathing so fast that he couldn't speak. His stomach was aching and his whole body trembled. At that moment he wanted to kill the boy at the computer. If he'd had had a pistol he would have killed him instantly, not with one shot but with forty. When his nerves were at their worst, he heard a voice telling him: "Ignacio, your breathing, concentrate on your breathing."

Immediately he remembered the master's message about concentrating on breathing any time he might have a crisis or important conflict. He began to take deep breaths, taking the energy of the breathing to an imaginary point in the middle of his forehead. After a few seconds he began to calm down. His breathing had slowed down enough for him to start his presentation. The assistant had the right picture on the screen.

Ignacio began, still nervous, in a hesitant tone of voice, but gradually he gained confidence. The people looked attentive and interested in what he was saying, and this attitude gave him the confidence to continue. Ignacio made a couple of comments that made the audience laugh. Seeing them relax gave him more confidence and he lost all his former nervousness. Ignacio threw himself into the task. As he gave his presentation, he thought constantly of giving the best of himself disinterestedly.

The most difficult part came. It was the point where Ignacio had planned to make those present meditate. For one second he thought: "I won't do it; nobody will realize and it'll be fine." But then he thought that if the true change comes through meditation, how could he be so selfish as to not have them meditate! He decided to do it. First he defended the advantages of meditation with studies from some major American universities. This persuaded the audience that meditation was not merely for half-naked people in India, and that it had proven benefits. He put on some soft music and made them concentrate on their breathing and keep their minds free from thoughts. He conducted the exercise for five minutes. At the end of the experience, the people were more relaxed and quiet. A better vibration could be felt in the atmosphere. Ignacio also meditated while he directed the exercise, as his master had always done. It was the first time he had done this and the sensation was much stronger than when he meditated alone. Directing the meditation magnified his feeling of well-being, as if someone were rewarding him for doing good. It filled him with happiness and love. He felt relaxed and happy. The time came to bring the presentation to an end; he told one of the master's meaningful stories and finished.

The people applauded with great enthusiasm. The applause did not stop; it lasted more than thirty seconds. While they applauded, Ignacio couldn't help shedding a few tears. He was full of emotion. He had managed to conquer his fears and he had given a lot of love. He felt very happy and fulfilled. He had never felt so whole as a person, nor had he ever seen his true mission in life with such clarity. He wanted to help the people in the business world to change, to live their spirituality, to live with a positive attitude. Now he knew that the master was not mistaken. He did have innate communication skills and he must use them to help people.

At the end of the presentation, dozens of people came up to Ignacio and thanked him sincerely. Each embrace, each handshake expressing thanks went straight to his heart. Only then did he understand the goal of life. "Service *is* what we come to this world for," he thought. The happiness he had felt was so great that his life would never be the same. Now he knew what really mattered.

When it was all over, his friend came up to him and said, "Ignacio, congratulations! I didn't know you were such a good speaker."

"To tell you the truth, I didn't, either," replied Ignacio.

"You didn't mention God in your presentation, but it's implicit in everything you said. I thought you were an atheist. Tell me, do you believe in God?"

Ignacio's first impulse was to reply, "Of course not." That had always been his answer in the past. He was used to the master speaking to him about The One. It didn't bother him any more, but for him to believe in God was another thing altogether. Nevertheless, the meditation, the time spent preparing the presentation, and the conference itself had made him experience a happiness that was not material. It was a divine sensation that took him closer to The One. He had never used the word The One. He felt strange saying it. But now he was sure that The One existed. He felt this every day when he was meditating. Ignacio replied:

"The truth is that I never thought that I believe in The One—or God as you call Him. But now I am sure The One exists."

Ignacio realized he had just burned all his bridges with this presentation—like an invading general making sure his troops could not turn back and must give their best to go forward to victory. He had revealed his interests in public, he had publicly affirmed that he believed in The One. His life was taking a new route, and he was the driver and passenger at the same time. Driver because he was there of his own free will, but passenger because part of him found it difficult to change, felt that everything was new, and was filled with uncertainty. He felt like going to find his master straightaway, to tell him about his success. But then he thought perhaps it was his ego that wanted to show how successful he was. He decided to go the following day, more calmly.

⌘

When he reached the master's house, he sat down quietly on his usual cushion and remained in silence.

"Aren't you going to tell me how you got on?" asked the master. "I haven't seen you for more than three months."

Ignacio smiled at him with gratitude.

"You know how I got on. You were there. You know that you saved me from dying when you reminded me about my breathing during the presentation."

"A good master never abandons his disciples," said the master.

"How did you manage to be there without your body?" asked Ignacio.

"I have told you before, that does not matter. The only thing I will remind you of is what you yourself have told me: on the spiritual plane we are all connected and we are all one. If something happens to you, it is as if it were happening to me."

"But I can't do that. I meditate every day but I can't make my consciousness travel outside my body like you can," replied Ignacio.

"And why would you want to do that? To feel powerful, magical, the chosen one, or to work in a circus? Ignacio, forget those foolish things and continue to concentrate on the meditation. Tell me, how do you feel today, now that the presentation is over?"

Ignacio had a reproach for the master. He felt that if he didn't tell him, he would burst.

"Before I say any more, I want to tell you that you deceived me. Your technique for getting rid of fear is no use at all. I nearly died. If it hadn't been for your advice to concentrate on my breathing, I would have had a heart attack."

The master, once more, had been expecting Ignacio's comment.

"Ignacio, the technique does work, and you must never stop using it. But every person is different. Speaking in public was more difficult in your case than for other people. Remember that you had a traumatic childhood; you had a father who pointed out all your mistakes and mistreated you. Standing up in front of the public, you turn every person present into a father who is going to scold you and punish you. Remember that in order to stop your parents from shouting at you and mistreating you, you tried to go unnoticed. Well, when you speak in public you are doing exactly the opposite. You become the protagonist who is in the limelight and you feel very frightened that you may be mistreated. I did not tell you the most important antidote to conquer fear, because if I had given you that antidote you would not have gone ahead with your presentation. You needed a technique to hang on to and feel secure, as if it were a life vest. The most important antidote to overcome fear is simply to confront it and to give the presentation. In other words, as in the story of the dog that I told you, you needed to be carried to the shore and dumped in the water. That is what happened to you. After that the dog had no problems drinking the water. You will not have any problems either when you next give your presentation. But I want to speak to you about a topic that has more to do with service."

The master paused, made his usual quiet movement while gathering up the folds of his fine tunic, and crossed his legs. Then he continued:

"A very rich Jew bought the best seat in the first row at the synagogue. He told the rabbi that he was donating that place so that someone who was unable to pay would be able to sit in a good place; he himself would sit at the back. The rich man sat at the back of the synagogue in such a way that he could be seen by everyone who passed forward to sit down. He wanted to be recognized for his generosity at all costs. Finally the rabbi said to him: 'It would be better if you sat in the front thinking that you would like to sit at the back, than to sit at the back thinking and showing with your attitude that you would like to sit in the front.' Ignacio, I want you to be careful not to do service with your ego. Do not let your ego manipulate you and give you away like the man in the story. Give of yourself, give service, give presentations, passing above your ego. The secret is to feel love and true dedication at every moment of your service."

Ignacio had already experienced that danger firsthand.

"I understand what you are telling me, Master. It isn't easy when people come up to you after the presentation to thank you. In fact, if you're not careful, the ego takes over."

"There are many, Ignacio, who engage in service like the rich man in the synagogue. They do it to stand out, to impress others as being generous, charitable people. But really they are looking for recognition, acceptance, and admiration to inflate their ego. Every time you give presentations, remember that the real reason for your presence is to help people to improve. As you become better known and more popular, it will become increasingly difficult to prevent your ego from manipulating you. As you achieve more successes, you will need to meditate more, so that your success does not make you feel superior. Now, Ignacio, you are ready for the fifth seed."

The master took out his box and gave Ignacio a seed wrapped in newspaper.

"Plant it. When it has grown, come back and we will talk about the message it holds."

⌘

Ignacio went home and stepped out into the garden. There he saw with nostalgia his whole evolution as a person. He saw the small hole left by the plant that never grew because it was the seed that had been crushed by a hammer, and he remembered how he had started discovering the blows of the hammer in his own past. Then he saw the Sensitive Plant, a beautiful flower that lives and is nourished in silence. He thought how the silence had helped him. He felt more tranquil, more at peace, happier, and above all, even though it seemed incredible to him, he now believed in The One. The rose tree looked beautiful; it had spread and had many roses. He remembered so many times when he had been the slave of his ego. He recalled how he had oriented his whole life to showing the world that he was the best, the most capable, and the most competent businessman. He remembered with humor how his ego had made him act and the problems it had caused him. He started to laugh at himself. Then he saw the small mango tree that in the future would give its fruits in service. He remembered the presentation, the enormous happiness he had felt when he had finally done something above himself.

Ignacio realized, after looking at his plants, that behind the lessons the master had wanted to give him, there were other lessons to be discovered. The slow growth of the plants represented the slow development that he was experiencing in each of the spiritual areas. Just as one could not speed up the growth of a plant, neither could one speed up one's learning process. He would have to be patient and accept the evolution of each stage. Besides, the plants were a living book for him. Looking at each one reminded him of all the master's teachings. It was like having him close by.

Full of emotion, he made a hole in the earth and planted the next seed. What new lesson would he learn? But he said to himself: "Patience, patience, Ignacio, that is what you have come to learn in this life."

The next day, as usual, he got up and started to meditate. He had increased his meditation time to forty-five minutes in the mornings, because he felt that this was the right amount of time to recharge his batteries of peace. When he finished, he took a shower and left for the office.

In the office he had an important strategic planning meeting with all his team. He wanted to finish the strategic plan ahead of time to be able to study the year's budget at depth. He had worked all day with his team and they still had a long way to go. That day was the birthday of Beatriz, the human resources manager, and the department had organized a little party for her with a cake, for six in the evening. When Ignacio's secretary called him and told him the people were outside waiting to start the celebration, he asked her to have them wait a little longer, and said that he and his team would be with them right away. But at six thirty the secretary interrupted him again to ask whether the party was to be canceled. Tense, with a worried expression on his face, he told his team:

"We'll have to stop, and we haven't finished yet, what a nuisance! The people have organized a party for Beatriz, and now we'll all have to go to it."

His gestures and his tone of voice showed that the party bothered him. He didn't want to stop for it. He thought that these events to sing "Happy Birthday" to people were a silly nuisance; he hated it when they did the same on his birthday.

"We'll go for a while and then come back to the meeting, OK?" said Ignacio, mortified.

At the party, Ignacio was in a hurry, looking at his watch all the time. He wanted them to sing "Happy Birthday" as soon as possible to go back to work. It was obvious that he was not enjoying the event. After ten minutes, he got his team together and asked them to come back to his office. As a special gesture of consideration, he told Beatriz to stay longer so that she could carry on enjoying herself at her party. Beatriz joined the meeting again after a while, but Ignacio noticed that she had a negative attitude and an angry expression. She had not said a single word. At eight, when his meeting was over and everyone had left, Ignacio went to look for Beatriz in her office and asked her:

"Beatriz, what's the matter? You haven't said a word. Did I do something to upset you?"

Beatriz remained silent. Something was obviously bothering her a lot. She had the expression of a person who is keeping back a flood of emotion.

"Tell me what I've done, please," insisted Ignacio.

"Perhaps the question should be what you haven't done," replied Beatriz.

Ignacio, beside himself with impatience, snapped back:

"Can you stop being so mysterious and tell me what on earth is the matter with you?"

Beatriz felt that things were going from bad to worse and decided to let it all out.

"The truth is that I feel I've been treated badly. You made the whole company wait half an hour for my birthday celebration. You leave the meeting reluctantly, hurry everybody up, and the message you put across to everybody is that none of this is of any interest to you whatsoever. You looked as if you had a train to catch the whole time. Ten minutes later, you take away the most important people in the company, because I am not valuable enough for you to spend more than ten minutes of your affection on me."

Ignacio could not believe that this was happening.

"I'm sorry, Beatriz. The thing is that this business of celebrating birthdays in the office, I just find it quite absurd and useless."

Beatriz's face was full of anger and pain.

"But of course, the only thing that matters is what is important for *you,* right? And the only thing that matters to you is things that have a purpose, practical things. Can't you ever stop being so selfish? Can't you think that perhaps birthdays do matter to me? Don't you realize that you are working with people, not machines? Don't you realize that besides a check at the end of the month people need your affection, your attention? Don't you realize that affection is shown in the little details, a smile, a 'thank you,' or a sincere congratulation to someone for her birthday?"

While Beatriz was speaking, Ignacio remembered the words of the master when he spoke about service: "Ignacio, service is not necessarily helping sick children or old folk; service means having a different attitude toward life. It means no longer thinking all the time of yourself but rather thinking of others, listening to them, taking them into account, being aware of their needs." He suddenly began to realize that with the incident of the birthday he was falling into the exact trap that he should have avoided. He realized that he was not capable of doing service in small things or taking other people into account in the details of daily life. That way he would never manage to turn his own life into an act of service.

He looked at Beatriz ruefully.

"You are so right! How stupid I've been! I don't know how I failed to realize. I'm very sorry," he said, and then added, like a mischievous child who wants to make up for his mistake: "Next year I promise that I'll be the one to organize your birthday!"

Beatriz was not expecting this reply. Ignacio had always made her feel ridiculous by making fun of her emotional weakness. But this time she was hearing a more humble, more sensitive Ignacio. She began to cry. . . . Ignacio consoled her for a few minutes and then went to the master's house. He felt like a crab, walking backward. The day before he had been proud of his progress, and now, just one day later, he felt a real failure because of the way he had behaved. Although the seed had not yet grown, he needed to see the master and tell him how bad he felt; but above all he hoped to discover the most intimate causes of his conduct, so that he would not make the same mistake again, because if after so much meditation he was still making mistakes, he couldn't be sure that the errors would not be repeated over and over again for the rest of his life.

This time he did not even stop to look at the small garden with its variety of new plants. He lacked inner peace, but it was like a vicious circle: he was upset because of his lack of peace, and this in turn prevented him from calming down and seeing things more clearly. When he was in the master's room, he barely greeted him before launching into a description of the birthday incident.

The master listened to him, expressionless. Then he imposed an eternal minute of silence. All that could be heard were the sounds of the breathing and the slightest sliding of the master's hands over the folds of his tunic. Then he commented:

"Ignacio, when you are going up in an airplane, have you never felt that the plane flies into an air pocket, a vacuum, and drops a few meters and then immediately rises again?"

"Yes, several times," replied Ignacio.

"The same thing is happening to you," continued the master. "In your vacuums of awareness you drop and feel that you are making a mistake. Then you recover your air or awareness and continue to fly gradually up again. Be patient. It seems that in the office you live with binoculars stuck to your eyes. You are so concentrated, looking at your targets and seeing how to approach them, that it is still difficult for you to see what is going on around you. Use the binoculars, they are necessary to set your direction, but take them away from your eyes to enjoy and love the people who work with you. Remember that the most important service you can give starts at home."

"But what can I do so that I won't forget? How can I remember to look around me? What can I do to stop being so self-centered?"

"Ignacio, both your eyes and your ears have been covered with a layer of wax. You used to see and hear yourself only in all your actions. Now, through meditation, the disinterested service and the fire of your soul that emerges to the surface will start melting this layer of wax and you will be able to listen more to the needs of the people around you. But you must be patient. Sometimes the longest road is the best one because it is the safest. The slow fire of your progress will gradually be melting the wax, and you have to be alert and patient."

Ignacio had calmed down. It was incredible the way that man had an answer to everything, but the most amazing thing was how he always had the most persuasive words on his lips.

"Tell me, has your seed grown yet?" asked the master.

"No, not yet, but I couldn't wait, I had to speak with you."

"Patience, Ignacio. Come back when you know what plant has grown from your seed, and what its teaching is."

CHAPTER SIX

The Sunflower Seed

The fifth seed was a sunflower. Not more than two months had gone by since sowing it, and a wonderful flower had bloomed, which turned its face to the sunlight during the day. Ignacio thought that the teaching must have something to do with the light. Perhaps it was the importance of orienting actions toward good, just as the sunflower oriented its flower toward the light.

But Ignacio was not paying much attention to the plant. Lately he had been very worried because, although his company was doing better, he needed to make a significant personnel reduction in order to keep it competitive. He had scheduled the reduction for four months later. His dilemma was whether to tell everyone about his decision straightaway, or to do it one week before asking the people to leave. It would be more considerate to give advance notice to those who were to be fired, so that they would be able to look for another job. Nevertheless, he was sure that the announcement of the "downsizing" would mean a big drop in the quality and productivity of the company. He was not sure what to do. He was thinking of consulting with the master.

That day he had an important meeting with Pedro, the marketing manager. He had been working on a very important sale for a government office. If he won it, that would mean a financial respite for the company. Pedro came into Ignacio's office radiating confidence and with a big smile.

"Ignacio, the government account is ours," he said.

"Great! What terms for us? When will they make their purchase? What amounts are we talking about?" asked Ignacio anxiously.

"If we make the sale, it will be the equivalent of 10 percent of our whole sales budget for the year. And believe it or not, they pay cash, as soon as we sign the contract and give them the bank guarantee."

"Right, what are we waiting for?" exclaimed Ignacio impatiently. "What's missing to close the deal?"

"The only thing that's missing is to confirm to the purchasing officer that we'll be giving him his cut."

At first, Ignacio was surprised.

"Wait a minute, do you mean a bribe?" he asked.

"Sure, like you've done other times with some of the State offices."

Ignacio wanted to tell him that he was no longer the same person as before, that now there were other things that mattered besides meeting goals. For example, his tranquility and peace of mind. Paying a bribe took away his tranquility and upset him. He had the feeling that it was not right, but at the same time he had doubts because he really needed those sales.

"If I did it once, that doesn't mean I have to do it all the time, does it?" objected Ignacio.

Pedro could not believe his ears.

"Oh come on, don't be a hypocrite," he said, with an expression of frustration on his face. "You know that in the State sector everyone pays a commission for this type of purchase. If you're not willing to pay up, then your competition will and they'll snatch the deal out of your hands. You don't know how difficult it's been for me to persuade the purchasing clerk to favor us. I've been working on this account for months. Can't you see that this is a war and all strategies are valid? We need to increase our profit. With this account we'll improve our financial statements and the banks will take the pressure off us. Just tell me the commission is OK and I'll see to it."

Ignacio wanted to gain time to ask the master's advice about this.

"Let me think about it. I'll answer you first thing tomorrow."

***

At the end of the day he went to the master's house. Once he was sitting on his cushion on the floor, he told the master about the dilemma of the commission and asked his advice.

"A mountaineer always has many possible ways to reach the top," commented the master. "Some slower, less steep, but safer. Others much shorter, steeper, and with a lot of loose ice. It is the same in the world of business. Just as your dilemma shows, you have several routes to reach the summit of your goals. Some faster, like paying dishonest commissions to third persons, and others relatively slower but safer in the long run, like basing your business conduct on ethics and values. Maybe the mountaineer will not fall this time if he takes the short-cut and is lucky. But I am sure that in the long run, if taking shortcuts becomes a habit for him, he will slip in the loose snow and put his life at risk. When we act against our values, the road is slippery too, and we can fall at any moment. Now, the choice of the route that the mountaineer is to take to the top of the mountain depends on his objective in climbing the mountain. If what he wants is to reach the top as quickly as possible, regardless of how he does it, perhaps he will take the risky shortcut. If his objective, on the other hand, is to enjoy each one of his steps in the ascent to the top, with peace, happiness, and tranquility, I am sure that he will take the sounder route."

The master stopped speaking for a few seconds. He changed his position on his cushion to a very upright one, and continued:

"Ignacio, we come back to the same question we have discussed before. What is your objective as you climb up to the summit of your life? To get there quicker? To go higher than anyone else? Or to live in peace and enjoy the route?"

At that moment, Ignacio had only one answer.

"We have talked about this before. A few months ago I would have said that the end justifies the means, and I wouldn't have hesitated about making the sale based on a bribe. But now, I am more and more convinced that my goal is to live in peace and tranquility. Bribing that person makes me feel dishonest and dirty, and that bothers me. The incredible thing is that I hardly recognize myself in this. For me, business was always business, and all means were valid as long as I won. It's as if before, I always had a little devil sitting on my shoulder and advising me on all my business decisions. Now there is a little angel, too, whispering in my other ear, and to tell the truth, it's not at all easy for me."

Once again, the master knew exactly what Ignacio meant.

"What has happened, Ignacio, is that meditating, giving service, and controlling your ego has brought out your own inner angel: your soul. It has made you develop your intuition and spirituality and enabled you to have the divinity present in all your decisions. The problem with ethical dilemmas is society accepts many kinds of conduct as valid even though they go against ethical principles. A typical case is the dilemma you have brought to me: to pay or not to pay bribes and commissions. Many people justify paying commissions with the argument that everyone does it, it's normal, it is the traditional way of doing business. In other words: 'If everyone does it, why shouldn't I?' Another accepted behavior that goes against values is, for example, buying stolen goods, especially car parts, or buying cheap illegal reproductions of books. The people who buy these articles do not even think that they are promoting dishonesty. In fact, they justify their conduct by saying: 'The other books are too expensive,' or 'Why should we pay the author if he already has too much money?' The types of conduct that are accepted by society cloud people's mental glasses, and they do not realize that they are acting against their values. I am sure that they expect their children to be honest and not tell lies, and they teach them not to steal, but they cannot see that when they buy a stolen article or an illegally produced book, they are stealing other people's rights."

Ignacio was astonished. First, the master had reflected about the business world as lucidly as he dealt with spiritual and psychological questions, and now he was moving into the field of ethics with an equally crystal-clear perception of things. The master continued:

"They say that an emperor once gave the order that all those who bought or accepted stolen merchandise be condemned to death, but he gave no sentence for thieves. All his people criticized him for acting irrationally. So the emperor took all the authorities to the coliseum. He put mice in the middle of the arena and threw pieces of cheese to them. The people were intrigued with the emperor; in fact, they thought he had gone crazy. When the mice saw the cheese, they took it and each one ran to its hole. The next day he gathered all the authorities in the coliseum again, and once more put mice in the middle of the arena, but this time he blocked the entrances to the mouse-holes. The mice took the cheese, but since they could not go into their holes to eat it, they left the cheese in its place and ran away. The emperor had shown that if there are no consumers of stolen goods, there will not be thieves either."

The master stroked his beard, took a breath, and continued explaining:

"Ignacio, if nobody bought illegally produced books, there would be no people making them. If nobody bought stolen articles, there would be fewer thefts. If nobody ever gave bribes, people would not ask for them. It is we ourselves who have fomented antivalues that are now accepted by all. We ourselves have darkened our mental glasses. We do not realize that in the long run every bribe we give or every dishonest act we perform affects all of society, and that includes ourselves.

Tomorrow you may be the victim of a bribe or a theft. Meditating and doing service has made your mental glasses cleaner and made it possible for you to question the ethical impact of situations."

Ignacio knew that the master was right in theory, but he did not understand how he himself, an entrepreneur inextricably involved in the battles of competition and survival, could stand aside from the real world to follow ethical principles. If everybody gave bribes, he would not survive by refusing to do so. It would greatly lessen his chances.

"It's difficult, Master, not to pay bribes," Ignacio said. "The company has such a lot to lose if I don't do it. . . ."

"On the contrary, your company has so much to lose if you *do* do it," replied the master.

"What do you mean?" asked Ignacio. He continued to see only too clearly the benefits he would obtain and how very much he would lose if he persisted in his scruples.

"A nugget of gold seen from afar looks like a little bean. A bean of gold one centimeter from your eyes looks like a big gold nugget. You are seeing close at hand all you can gain by paying the bribe, but in reality you are seeing only the little gold bean. You are so desperate to gain that little gold bean that you do not see in the distance the large gold nugget that you will obtain by not paying commission. Learn to analyze the consequences of your acts and to see the complete picture. Be aware of all that you can lose by giving that commission and value all that you can gain as a person and as a company by acting according to your principles."

"If I don't pay the commission, all I can gain is greater moral tranquility. What else can I gain?"

The master shook his head at him, with that typical gesture of sadness of someone who sees things clearly, when the other person insists on making mistakes.

"Very simple, Ignacio. First of all, think of the negative consequences. Have you ever thought that they may discover that your company has paid bribes and, in the best of cases, there will be a report in the media? They could create a bad image for you in the community. And in the worst case, they could put you in prison for committing a crime. When your company pays bribes, you are sending a message to your whole organization: 'Here we value dishonesty, cheating on the system, deception, and accepting bribes.' Do you want your own people to accept bribes and make you buy articles of poor quality from corrupt suppliers?

"Ignacio, remember that it is your actions that define the values of your organization, not your words. You can talk all you want about the value of honesty, but if you do not show it with your acts, it will never permeate your company. How much does your company stand to lose from theft, bribery, and cheating? On the other hand, look at all you have to gain by not paying that bribe. Besides being more at peace with yourself and satisfied with your decision, you will be giving an example of congruence to your whole organization. You will increase people's trust in you as a leader, you will educate your staff to respect the values that you really want in your company, but above all you will be aligning your organization with the light; you will be acting with the values of the soul, and by the law of karma, you will obtain better results. You will obtain the nugget of gold, not the gold bean. Now tell me, Ignacio, do you not think you have much more to lose by paying the bribe?"

Ignacio had stopped being obstinate. Really, deep down in his soul, since the beginning of this dialogue, all he had wanted was to get to the bottom of this matter.

"I had never thought of the consequences in that way."

"When race horses are competing, they are blinkered to shut out their lateral vision. The jockey wants his horse to look ahead all the time, toward the finishing post, and not to be distracted by looking to the sides. It is the same with executives: they have their blinkers on, so that they can look only at their goals and obtain results. When making their decisions, they leave aside human aspects and values because their mental blinkers do not allow them to see the whole picture. Ignacio, take off your blinkers and you will see the true reality. You will see that it is not a case of one road only to reach the goal."

Ignacio was surprised by the profound ethical thought of the master. All these topics were very new to him. Ethics and business had always been two facets of his life that he had kept completely apart. Ignacio was becoming aware that he had lived by a double standard of conduct. Ethics was for the home, for friends and family. In business, on the other hand, everything was permitted, and the only use for values was to hang them in cute frames in the managers' offices. He suddenly had a feeling of uncertainty; he felt quite upset. He thought: "How many times must I have put my foot in it because of having my mental blinkers on, and not acting according to my principles?"

Ignacio remembered that he wanted to ask the master for advice about another dilemma in the company: whether or not to inform the employees in advance about the personnel reduction. Ignacio gave the master the details. The master listened carefully, but instead of answering, he asked another question:

"Tell me, Ignacio, do you know now what plant the last seed I gave you is?"

"It's a sunflower. I had the idea that it must be something to do with orienting your actions or your life toward the light, toward The One."

"That's right, but before your actions come your decisions. The sunflower reminds us that it doesn't matter what circumstances or problems we face in life, or at what time of the day we find ourselves, we must always orient our decision toward the light, toward The One. We should always seek to have the light illuminate our way. In all moral dilemmas, of necessity different values confront each other; you will have to decide on whichever road is closest to the essence of your spirit."

"But how can I know which roads are closest to my spirit?"

The master stood up very slowly, speaking all the time. Suddenly, since Ignacio nearly always saw him sitting down, he seemed to Ignacio larger than expected, although he saw straight away that his stature was that of an average man. But his image, seen from the cushion, wrapped in his words, made him look immense.

"It is not easy, but you can take certain criteria into account. For example, in any dilemma, try to identify which of the two alternatives benefits or helps the greater number of people or at least minimizes their suffering. Remember that we all come from the same source and in reality we are all one. To seek the happiness of the greatest number of individuals is aligned with spirituality. Another way to tackle the dilemma is to remember the innate qualities of the spirit: peace, love, joy, compassion, dedication, and kindness. Evaluate which of the ways of solving the dilemma is more oriented toward these qualities. We often find instrumental values, like efficiency and profitability, in confrontation with the values of the spirit. In these cases, do not lose sight of the fact that the true goal in life is to develop your spirit and that business is not the end but the means to achieving an end. Finally, you can use the Golden Rule: 'Do as you would be done by.' This law again leads us to the spiritual concept of our all being one. For example, in the dilemma you have described to me, what values are at stake?"

"In the case of the dismissals," replied Ignacio, "perhaps the values confronting each other are the profitability and efficiency of the company, if I don't communicate the personnel reduction in advance, and the values of compassion, love, respect, and loyalty to my employees."

"Which decision, Ignacio, do you believe will benefit more people or reduce the suffering of more people? And if you were in the shoes of the people in question, how would you like to be treated? Which path do you think is more aligned with the innate qualities of the soul? Which path represents the sunflower's movement toward the light?"

"That's obvious, Master, but once more I have to sacrifice the company's productivity if I am to act ethically."

The master sat down on the cushion again, and crossed his legs.

"Imagine that you are driving on a highway and you go over a stone that hits your oil tank and damages it. If you don't take any notice and keep going at top speed, I am sure that you will advance some kilometers, but then the engine will seize up. If you stop and fix the oil leak, the car will respond and carry you a long way farther. In a company, trust is like oil for the engine of a car. If there is no trust, all you will have is friction, conflicts, and wear and tear. Everything is slower, more costly, and the organization ends up stalling. If you tell your personnel only one week in advance that you are thinking of dismissing them, you are really communicating another more significant message: you are telling all those who remain in the company that they cannot trust you. That tomorrow the same thing may happen to them, and that they might be dismissed from your organization when they least expect it. You are teaching them, with your acts, that the values you believe in are lying, manipulation, lack of respect, disloyalty, and selfishness. Again you are concentrating on the gold bean, worried about the costs of lowering productivity for a four-month period, but you do not realize the enormous cost that a lack of trust can cause your company.

"Look at all you have to lose. Imagine you go into a boardroom that has a big pane of glass separating it from another room. If the glass were a mirror, you would not know whether someone was looking at you from the other side. If the glass were dark, you would just about manage to make out what was going on in the other room. At least you would know that something was going on. Finally, if the glass were transparent, you would be able to see everything that was happening in the other room. The question is: which gives you the most confidence?"

"The room with the transparent wall, of course" replied Ignacio.

"Ignacio, a leader has to be like a transparent pane of glass and not hide anything from his people. If you have some problem or difficulty, if you have to make decisions with serious consequences, you must share them with them. Nurturing trust in your organization will be your greatest asset. So, to sum up: when you are faced with a business decision that presents you with a moral dilemma, first understand the problem properly and define which values are at odds. Then analyze the positive and negative consequences of each decision. Do not stay in the short term; think of the long-term results. Do not limit yourself to analyzing only the economic results; think also about the real message you will be giving with your actions. Then define which of the two alternatives of the dilemma maximizes the happiness or minimizes the suffering of a greater number of people. Analyze which alternative is better aligned with the qualities of the soul, of love and compassion. Ask yourself: if you were in the place of the main actor in the problem, how would you like to be treated? Finally, ask your spirit and your intuition which alternative will let you sleep better at night or look at yourself in the mirror every day."

Ignacio felt that he should make full use of the master's approaches, so he was not content with giving easy answers. He preferred to bring all his arguments out, in order to go deeper into the problem. He knew that only a perfect understanding could lead him to prevent later errors.

"But supposing that even with all this analysis I can't decide on one of the—" he started to ask.

The master cut him short, as if he already had the answer on the tip of his tongue.

"Then learn to get out of the dilemma and find other alternatives with creativity. Make it into a trilemma or a quadrilemma. For example, in the case of laying off personnel, you need to reduce costs and only see two possibilities: either you tell the people in advance about their dismissal, or you tell them one week beforehand. But why get stuck in that dilemma?

Have you not thought of the possibility of speaking with the people and offering them a third option?"

Ignacio was amazed at the direction the master's reasoning was taking.

"But what else can I do? I don't have any other alternatives."

"Why don't you propose a salary reduction for all the personnel, just for a time, without dismissing anyone? That would save money for your company."

Suddenly Ignacio felt that he could not understand how he himself, an experienced entrepreneur, son and grandson of entrepreneurs, had not managed to glimpse a practical solution like that. And yet, here was this gray-bearded man, with his eternally crossed legs and orange tunic, who was able not only to guide him through the spiritual world but also to come up with effective ways for him to tackle his conflicts in the company.

"Master, you speak as if you knew the world of business organizations very well. How come?"

The master hardly ever laughed, but this time he smiled as spontaneously and innocently as a child. While he listened to the reply, Ignacio was thinking that nothing revealed so clearly the cleanliness of a person's soul as the quality of his smile.

"The fact that I am in the spiritual world does not mean that I haven't had experiences in other areas," said the master, to Ignacio's surprise. "Companies and corporations are made up of people, the essence of people is the spirit, and that is my specialty."

"That's true," continued Ignacio, without failing to notice that in the master's words there was something more. "The alternative of reducing salaries is something I hadn't thought of. I'll evaluate it."

The master spoke again:

"The first four seeds that we worked with have served us to help bring your spiritual essence to the surface, to connect you with your soul and for you to feel your peace and happiness. The sunflower seed, about making ethical decisions, goes one step further. It is intended to help you live your life incorporating your essence into each of your acts. In other words, first we have worked on cleaning your inner lightbulb so that it will shine and give light. Now, the sunflower seed allows us to take your light down your road in life, making sure that the path is lit."

The master stood up and went to a table where there was a jug of orange juice, a strainer, and a glass. He poured the juice from the jug into the glass, filtering it through the strainer. He showed Ignacio the strainer:

"Look at all the impurities in the juice that were left in the strainer. Now I can enjoy the juice better."

The master left the glass on the table and continued:

"Ignacio, use the values of your spirit like this strainer for the different decisions that you have to make throughout your life. Do not let any decision through that is not aligned with your values. Enjoy the peace and tranquility—and harvest the fruits—of living ethically."

The master took out his box of seeds and handed one, wrapped in newspaper as usual, to Ignacio. He concluded:

"This seed will take quite some time to germinate and grow. It will give you a good time to practice everything you have learned. Meditate every day and apply everything I have taught you. When you know what the plant is, come back to discuss its message."

While Ignacio was driving home he thought about his conversations with the master. He hardly recognized himself; he was so surprised to find himself reflecting about work ethics and values. . . . He was himself, but it felt as if everything were happening to another person. There was still a rational side of himself that led him to doubt all these things. He wondered: "Perhaps I'm letting myself be influenced too much by all this? Perhaps I'm wasting my time with all these foolish things?" But the other side of his conscious mind—his intuition and his spirit, which had already gained a good deal of ground—told him that he was on the right path and that he should keep moving straight ahead.

CHAPTER SEVEN

The Seed of Balance

He had tried to incorporate the secret of the sunflower seed into his life. When decisions had to be made in the office, he no longer considered only economic aspects or results; he also evaluated whether the decision was aligned with the light. He reflected on ethics and was careful to filter out actions that did not respond to his deepest-felt values. Ignacio felt that life always offered him several alternatives when he had to make decisions, which could lead him to different roads. It was he who had to decide among the many options and open the door of the option that matched the key of his values. He just had to give himself the time necessary to try the key in the different doors, reflect ethically, and then decide.

Ignacio had continued to give presentations. His topic, spirituality in business, was so novel that company executives liked it a lot. Ignacio didn't charge anything; this was his service, his *dharma*. When he gave the presentations he felt very happy and fulfilled. At the end of the presentations several executives asked him to guide them onto the spiritual road. He was now clear about his mission in life: it was to bring spirituality to the business world.

Ignacio had noticed that all his modern books on leadership and management were in line with the age-old teachings of his master. Topics such as self-directed teams, empowerment, interpersonal communication, and change were closely linked with the spiritual approach. For example, teamwork called for giving up one's own interests and instead supporting the goals agreed on by consensus. It required not looking for people to blame, but rather helping people do a better job. This simply meant assuming an attitude of service and preventing the ego from taking control. The attitude of service came naturally when one meditated and gradually reduced one's ego. In the case of empowerment, so fashionable in the business world, in order to empower others the person must first be willing to transfer power. He had to stop thinking only of himself and see the benefits for the company and for the person being empowered. To effect empowerment, one had to trust, train, and help; and above all not be addicted to power. Again, in Ignacio's opinion, everything boiled down to an attitude of service and love toward others. If a person really wanted others to grow and develop, he would have no problems with empowerment.

Although he was meditating daily, Ignacio was stressed out at the office these days. He was clear about his mission in life and wanted to dedicate time to it. However, business crises, problems, and opportunities also took up a lot of time. There was so much he wanted to do but the day was not long enough, and he felt completely tense and out of control. Ignacio wanted to do everything: manage his company, give his presentations, design new ones, participate in congresses and interviews, write articles, spend time with his wife and children, have business meetings, and take part in boards of directors, and he simply could not cope with everything. He spent Saturdays and Sundays working, and those who suffered the most were his family.

Six months had passed since Ignacio had planted the last seed—a long wait. Every morning he visited the place, but there was nothing to be seen. He supposed that part of the teaching of the seeds was to learn to be patient, but he was finding it very difficult. Suddenly, that morning, a tiny shoot was visible. His gardener told him it was a little pine tree.

Since he would be seeing the master that day, he planned to be extra aware of each activity he undertook that day at work to identify where his problem was and then consult with the master.

He reached the office. He had a one-hour meeting planned with the finance manager to look at the cash flow.

"How are we doing? Everything going well?" asked Ignacio, while the manager took a seat in front of his large desk. It was one of those ultramodern tables. That and his comfortable revolving chair seemed to set up a barrier of superiority between the boss and whoever he was talking to. From there it gave the impression that the boss was able to control everything, as if he were in the cabin of a ship.

The manager looked at him seriously but enthusiastically.

"It's all going according to plan, but the thing is quite . . ."

"Just a minute, excuse me," interrupted Ignacio, when the phone rang.

After a couple of minutes, they started going over the cash flow. Ignacio's chair swiveled ceaselessly, to the right to look at data on the computer screen and then to the left to answer the never-ending telephone calls. Time seemed to fly for Ignacio; however, for the manager it was going at a snail's pace. Ignacio was like a busy ant dealing with a hundred questions at the same time, while the manager waited during each interruption, and they had still not been able to finish with the cash flow.

Fifteen minutes before the end, the marketing manager came into the office.

"Here are the texts of the press releases. Give them a quick look over," he said to Ignacio rather brusquely.

Ignacio had, indeed, asked to look at them, and he took a long time checking line by line and making suggestions. Finally he remembered that he had an appointment with a client. He had not yet finished with the press releases. He asked the finance manager to plan another meeting for the next day so that they could finish going over the cash flow.

When he reached the client's office, it was half an hour later than the time they had agreed on. He had gone into another meeting, but he accepted Ignacio's invitation to have lunch with him. Ignacio had arranged to have lunch with his family that day, so he had to call home to cancel that arrangement. He waited for an hour with nothing to do. Then he went to lunch with the client.

When he arrived back at his office after lunch, he decided to invest his time helping the graphic designer to prepare the art for an ad. Ignacio loved marketing, creating ads . . . he enjoyed using the design software on the computer. But his specialty was producing creative headlines for the campaigns. He had spent three hours there, when his logistics manager came to look for him and interrupted him.

"Ignacio, an international supplier has called to confirm whether the launch of his product will be next week."

The production manager knew nothing about it, he said. Ignacio jumped up from his seat, distraught.

"Oh shit! That's right! I'd completely forgotten to schedule it! It's incredible how something so important——" But the phone rang and Ignacio picked it up, while the designer and the logistics manager exchanged a silent look.

They spent the rest of the afternoon developing a mediocre emergency plan to get themselves off the hook. But Ignacio had promised to give a presentation in a company and he had to leave to get there on time. They had not finished the emergency plan. He put the drafts in his briefcase to work on later that night, and rushed off to the presentation venue. The presentation was a success.

At about eight o'clock he went to the master's house. While he drove he was thinking that he did not have his life under control. He felt like a puppet, manipulated entirely by circumstances. It was obvious that he had spent the whole day as if he were caught in a spider's web. The more he moved, the worse he entangled himself, without managing to finish anything off. He knew that the meditation helped him, calmed him down, but when he was in the office it was a nonstop merry-go-round, and it was impossible for him to control it.

Ignacio was happy to see the master. He really missed him. The six months had seemed interminable to him. He told him about his frustration over the way he was managing his time and he described what he had done that day.

"Master, I really sense that I lack integrity. In my talks I tell people to meditate in order to live in peace and tranquility, but I live stressed out because there's not enough time. I haven't stopped meditating, and I feel that the meditation has made me a better person, but at the office I can't seem to be at peace."

"Ignacio, come into the garden with me," was all the reply he obtained from the master, who stood up calmly and waved him toward the garden.

They both went out into the garden. The master gave him a square plastic jug.

"Fill this jug with water and water that palm tree," said the master, pointing to a small palm tree beside the door.

Ignacio did not understand why the master was making him water plants when what he needed was answers to his questions. But he knew him by now; he liked to teach with analogies. Ignacio had learned to learn with this methodology. He liked it very much, because that way the concepts were engraved on his mind. Ignacio took the jug, filled it with water, and walked to the palm tree. But the jug was cracked, so the water leaked out and very little reached the plant.

Ignacio suspected that it was not a simple crack in the jug. "He didn't bring me into the garden for no reason at all," he thought, chuckling to himself. He had gradually come to realize that with the master the words and objects soon ended up in the realm of allegory, that is, each word and each object belonged to a symbolic register from which some lesson could be extracted. Nevertheless, he decided to follow the path where the master was leading him step by step.

"Master, the jug is cracked. Don't you have another one to water the plant?" asked Ignacio.

The master knew that his disciple had learned to wait for his teaching.

"Ignacio, it is the same with human beings. All human beings have a jug of water, which is their lifetime on this plane. They decide how to use it. Some waste it by simply throwing the water of time away in the desert; that is, they devote their lives to insignificant activities that do not bring happiness or peace. Others, like you, do orient their lives toward significant activities, in line with what they really want for their existence. That is to say, instead of throwing the water away in the desert, they use it to water the palm tree. The problem of the majority is that their jug is so badly cracked with time-wasting that they have little time to dedicate to important activities. In other words, what happened to you when you tried to water the palm tree."

Ignacio always felt he was being outwitted if there was something he could not quite grasp.

"Excuse me, Master, but I don't waste my time. I work twelve hours a day. My problem is that I have too much work."

"With the jug cracked, you can work twelve hours and even so you will not finish watering the plant. It is not a question of how many hours of work, but of how you use them. The problem with you is that your time-wasting is disguised as something important, because of its urgency. You realized clearly that the jug was cracked; you saw the water running out and you were aware of the problem. With time-wasting, it is really very difficult to see what is happening. We believe that the water of time is falling onto important activities, but in fact it is not."

"But tell me, how have I wasted my time? Everything I have done today is important."

"First let us define what is important for you. What is your *dharma* or mission in this life, what do you really want to attain by the end of your life on this plane?"

Ignacio felt confused again.

"Well, we've talked about this before," he replied. "I believe it has something to do with helping to spiritualize the business world. Helping executives to realize how important it is to live in peace and happiness, regardless of the circumstances. Making them see the happiness to be obtained by disinterested service and dedication."

The master made a slow pause, as if he were leaving space for Ignacio to think about his own words.

"If you really want to teach the importance of living in peace, are you doing it? What example are you giving to the executives in your company, who see you rushing desperately from one appointment to another, stressed out and distraught? Are you really teaching peace and happiness regardless of the circumstances?"

Ignacio looked at the master like a docile pupil. He felt very small and ignorant. The master, once again, had made him aware that he was not yet fully aware, that he still had a lot to learn.

"It's true, like this I am not fulfilling my *dharma*," replied Ignacio dejectedly.

"Ignacio, it is clear that for you your company is a means and no longer an end in itself. Your company offers you an interesting environment with challenges that allow you to grow. It is, indeed, difficult to remain in peace and happiness in such an environment. But the purpose of it all is for you to develop as a person so that you can be an example to others and serve others. Devote time to what is important, Ignacio. Try to delegate to other people the greatest number of routine activities in which you do not contribute a value. Place your trust in them and train the persons who work with you to decide things for themselves. Don't act as the savior of the world, spurred on by your ego. Do not try to deceive yourself into believing that if you don't do things yourself, everything turns out wrong. Be careful with interruptions. One of your main problems is that everybody interrupts you. Our ego tends to be very pleased with the idea that we are the most important, the most consulted, those who have all the answers and solutions. Deep down, our ego is delighted that we are constantly being interrupted, but this means that we are taking valuable time away from the supply our spirit needs to fulfill its *dharma*."

Ignacio found it difficult to imagine that things would work without his omnipresence.

"But, Master, my people need me; if I don't help them with their decisions, the company comes to a full stop."

The master pointed to the palm tree that remained beside them, unwatered because of the cracked jug.

"I believe that you need them more than they need you. Learn to release the egoistic power that wants to be the focus of everything. Train and help your people caringly so that they will be able to make decisions and work on their own initiative without needing you. Give them the water of your trust so that they may grow.

"A woman once came to ask my advice about her five-year-old son, who was very dependent on her: he wanted to go everywhere with her, he would not leave her in peace. The little boy was very immature for his age; he wanted to be carried around like a baby. I asked her: 'Do you want to have a baby or a boy?' The woman was upset with my question: 'Why do you think I'm here?' she said, angrily. 'You are here to sort out your little boy's problem, not to hear what you want to hear,' I replied to her. I explained that unconsciously it was she who was creating the dependency, and that deep down inside her she did not want her son to grow, she wanted to continue having him at her side, feeling needed and important.

"Ignacio, the same thing is happening to you in the office with your subordinates." The master paused. "Female eagles," he continued, "first teach their offspring to fly by example. The baby eagle learns by observing while it grows and becomes stronger. The mother observes the weight of her eaglet, the number and length of its feathers, and when she senses that it is ready, she pushes it out of its nest into the big empty sky. The eaglet is forced to open its wings and fly. Then the mother follows it closely to help it if it gets into problems, but at a distance so that the eaglet will not depend on her. Nature is very wise. Follow the steps of the eagle with your people: prepare them, train them, then launch them into their own space so that they will fly by themselves. Stay near them, but at the same time keep your distance, to help them to continue growing and become independent."

Ignacio recognized once more that the master's vision was irrefutable.

"I agree, if I really make an effort I can delegate a lot of my work," he said. "Perhaps that will give me a bit more time, but I don't think it will be enough. I feel that I don't have enough time even to do all the important things. I want to design and deliver presentations on spirituality. I want to make my company successful so that it will be an example. I would love to write about these topics. I want to help people. I want to be with my family. I need to exercise and I never can. I don't have time for it all."

The master gestured for Ignacio to follow him indoors.

"I imagine that you already know what plant grew from the last seed you planted."

"Yes, it's a pine, but I haven't the slightest idea what its lesson could be."

"What do you think is special about a pine?" asked the master, looking steadily at him and placing his long hands on his knees.

"Its height?" Ignacio replied, uncertain.

"That's right. That is one of its characteristics, but what makes the pine special is the symmetry of its branches. It is a perfectly symmetrical tree. This gives it an excellent equilibrium, which enables it to grow very tall and remain completely balanced. Also, if you climb to the top of a pine and look down, you will see a solid green mass. Each branch is placed in such a way that it does not overshadow any other branch; in this way it maximizes the absorption of solar energy. Finally, in winter, in the northern areas when the pine is full of snow, the form of its leaves prevents snow from accumulating, which might make the pine lose its natural balance. Unlike other trees, the pine lets most of the snow pass down through it, thereby preventing its possible collapse from excess weight."

The master paused before continuing.

"And now, do you understand what the message could be?" Seeing that Ignacio was still not sure, he explained: "The message of wisdom that the pine holds for us is the message of perfect balance in life. We, like the pine, also have branches, that is to say, the different roles we play in the drama of our life. For example, you are the manager of your company, but you are also a father and a son. You play the role of friend, you have started playing the role of conference speaker, and you want to play the role of writer. The secret, Ignacio, is that you must try to balance each branch or each role you play in your life, to achieve a perfect equilibrium. You must try to make sure that in the long term one role does not overshadow another, just as the pine manages its branches: they all receive the same amount of sun's energy. Finally, in each role in your life you will come across difficulties and obstacles. Instead of becoming distraught and bearing the burden of the problems, learn from the pine to remain always lightweight. Let the weight of the snow of the problems pass through, so that you can always keep your balance and continue growing. Plan each week in such a way that you give time to your different roles in life."

Ignacio felt that the road was becoming increasingly difficult. But at the same time he felt capable of overcoming the obstacles.

"There will be weeks," continued the master, "in which circumstances will oblige you to spend more time on one role only, but in the long run you should balance your time among them all. It is like a juggler who has several rods with plates on them: he has to keep them all spinning, otherwise they will lose their speed and fall off. If only one of the plates is spinning, the rest will end up on the ground. Each role you play in life is like one of those plates. If you do not keep them all spinning, one of them will end up on the ground."

"Yes, I agree, I have all those roles to play," interrupted Ignacio, "but I wouldn't know where to start to imitate the pine's equilibrium."

"Start by making sure that you invest your time in what is really important, and by not letting yourself be carried away by the currents and whirlpools of urgency. Learn to say no to interruptions and to work that you may like doing, but to which you do not contribute a significant value. Stop attending each and every meeting, trust your staff, and try to delegate as much as possible in order to concentrate on what you really want to achieve in life."

Ignacio sometimes had the impression, when he heard the master handling things in this way, that this man, once the spiritual sessions were over, hurried away to submerge himself in the turbulence of a secret company, where he managed everything to perfection and knew how to tackle every problem.

"Master, you speak to me as if you knew, as if you had lived through all this before, as if you had managed companies yourself. Can that be so?"

"Everything is possible," said the master, with a smile of acknowledgment. "This advice I am giving you is merely common sense from the point of view of a person looking at your problems from the outside."

The master then asked Ignacio to go with him to the kitchen. This was the first time that Ignacio had been anywhere in the house apart from the consulting room or the garden. He was immediately struck by the cleanliness of the place, the strange shapes of some of the pans and utensils, and the enormous number of spices and small jars of tea in perfectly straight rows. The master put a kettle on the stove, and when the water boiled, he said:

"Try to get hold of the steam coming out of the spout."

Ignacio didn't even try.

"Master, that's impossible. Nobody can take hold of steam."

"Try, anyway," urged the master.

Ignacio approached the kettle and with a resigned gesture tried in vain to catch hold of the steam.

"Now, Ignacio, try to catch this water from the tap with your hand."

The master opened the faucet of the sink, and Ignacio tried to catch the water with his hand.

"It's impossible, too, unless I have a bowl or cup. I can only keep a few drops in my hand."

Finally, the master took some ice cubes out of the refrigerator and asked Ignacio to try and catch them as he dropped them. Ignacio caught all the ice cubes easily. He knew that something important was hidden behind those maneuvers, but he could not quite see what it was.

"Time is like water," said the master, while he served tea in two small cups. "When you live for urgent things only, your time evaporates like boiling water and it is impossible for you to retain it for important activities. When you are more aware of the need to concentrate on important activities and you stop spending all your time on urgent things, it is liquid, like water: it still slips through your fingers, but you are able to hold back a few drops. Finally, when you make blocks with your time and you separate it for important activities, it is like ice cubes—you really have the control in your hands. The advice I want to give you, Ignacio, is that you should divide your week into compartments. Freeze the time in blocks for your important activities. Otherwise, time will evaporate like steam."

Ignacio understood the meaning of all that, but he needed something more specific.

"But what do you mean when you say 'compartments' and 'freezing' my time?"

"For example, if you want to give presentations, allocate a couple of fixed days a week at specific times; the same if you want to write. Schedule a time and hour just for thinking and another for working on pending matters and important things. If you consider that visiting your company's best clients is important, schedule a fixed time in the week for that. If you block out your week for really important activities, you will keep aligned with your real mission in life, Ignacio. Needless to say, this only works if you respect it. I would recommend that you give a copy of your timetable to all your company executives, so that they know which times are reserved.

"Do not set aside all the hours of the week, because that doesn't work. You need free time and time available for your personnel to consult with you, for different meetings, or simply to take care of unforeseen matters. Ignacio, the human being undertakes the journey of his life in a canoe from the top of a lake; he follows the course of a river, and always ends up in the ocean, flowing into unity with The One. How he decides to travel and invest his time depends on the person alone. Some love spending their time in the rapids of the river, even if the rapids might crash them against the rocks. They enjoy the adrenaline. They spend their whole life going as fast as possible and think that their goal in life is to overcome the rocks and obstacles. Others decide to have a more peaceful life. They steer their canoe to avoid the rapids. They stop to rest in the lakes formed by the river and understand that their objective is to enjoy traveling happily and peacefully. Both types of people reach the ocean of The One at the end of their lives. Which group do you want to be in?

"The answer is obvious. I can't think of any human being who would not want to live in peace and happiness, without risking colliding against rocks. But the thing is that the whole system we live in leads us to believe that the goal is to go faster, to obtain better results, more prestige and success.

"It is difficult, indeed, to break a habit. You have lived your life as if you were in the first canoe. From that canoe it is difficult to see the opportunities to dodge the rapids and move to calmer areas. You need to be very much aware all the time. From now on, Ignacio, every weekend you will plan the coming week by allocating time to the different roles you play in life. You will block out your week so that nobody can invade your zones of important activities, such as those linked with your *dharma* and the practice of meditation. At the end of the week you will make an in-depth evaluation of how you got on, and you will get better and better at it."

"I really want to make a start on this planning," said Ignacio. "I have never done it the way you describe. I think that with this I'll manage to bring balance into my life."

The master took a last long sip of tea, looked at Ignacio again, and replied:

"Not necessarily. You are lacking a very important element. It would be impossible for the pine to achieve its perfect balance if it were not nourished with clean water and the right nutrients. Otherwise, any wind could blow it over. Ignacio, The One has given you a body to carry out your *dharma* in this life, and you have to take care of it. Your body is like a vehicle and your spirit is the driver. If you feed it with impure, low-octane fuel, you will not get very far. You need to understand the different types of foodstuffs and their impact on your body."

Ignacio felt disoriented again, because once more the master had taken him by surprise. This man seemed to have a strict plan for him, a plan of salvation that he was putting into practice little by little, finding the appropriate time for each lesson.

"There are three types of foods," continued the master, seeing Ignacio's surprised expression, "*tamasic, rajasic,* and *satvic.* Tamasic foods are those that make you sleepy and lazy; they lead to inaction, inertia, and heaviness. They are, for example, food kept for more than one day, canned food, cured cheeses, overcooked food that is dry and without juices, red meat, wines, alcoholic drinks, and also tobacco. Rajasic foods are those that lead you to act all the time; they produce euphoria, energy, aggressiveness, they fill you with thoughts, distress, and preoccupations. Rajasic foods have many spicy condiments, mustard, chili peppers, pickled gherkins, garlic, and onions; in this group we also have coffee, fish, and chicken. Finally, the satvic foods are those that produce balance and peace and increase your vitality and strength. These foods produce happiness, clarity, and balance; they are like affection for the stomach. They are the vegetables, fruit, nuts, fresh food, dairy products, butter, soft cheeses, and cereals. As a general rule, you should try to eliminate the tamasic foods. You should eat a moderate percentage of rajasic foods. The rajasic foods give you energy and stimulate you to action. In the kind of life you lead, you need some of these foods to stimulate your will. But you should concentrate on the satvic foods for your nourishment. That will give you more balance, peace, and equilibrium."

Suddenly this seemed to Ignacio as great a challenge as the former ones.

"But how difficult, Master! I love red meat, and how boring to have to eat lettuce every day! But the hardest thing will be to give up coffee. I drink at least six cups a day in the office, and about ten sodas that have caffeine in them."

"With regard to coffee, you decide," replied the master. "If you want peace, that amount of caffeine will not help you. When you drink a lot of caffeine, it is very difficult to concentrate on meditation. I know that you have been doing it, but if you gave up caffeine you would feel the difference. The diet that I propose can be very pleasant if you learn to prepare and combine the foods. These are just recommendations, Ignacio. It depends on you if you want to live in balance, with a healthy body, with a dignified old age, and above all with more peace."

Ignacio felt that the cost was increasingly high. The master appeared to read his mind.

"The cost is far higher when you have an irreversible health problem due to bad eating habits. What you should do is simply be more conscious of what you are eating and stop giving such importance to the pleasures of the stomach. In the West, you reward those people known as *gourmands* with your admiration; you distinguish them for eating an enormous amount of foods that are destructive for the body. What you eat should not be a status symbol for society to see; rather, it should be a private choice to seek greater balance in life.

"The story goes that a prince, out hunting with his hawk, was very thirsty. For two whole days they had not found a pond of water to drink from. Finally, high on a mountain, they saw a small lake. They climbed up. The prince took out his cup while the hawk flew after prey. When the prince was about to drink the water from his cup, the hawk swooped down and struck it from his hand with its talon, so that he could not drink. Once more, the prince tried to drink, but the same thing happened again. The prince, tired of the hawk, took out his sword, planning to kill it if it spilled the water again. He was about to drink for the third time, when he saw the hawk swooping down at him again. He took out his sword and killed it, but the hawk's strong talons had already tossed the cup up into the air. The prince had to climb up to a large rock where the cup had landed, and when he picked it up, he saw another small lake that fed the one where he had been, and it had a dead venomous snake in it. Then he understood what his companion, the hawk, had been trying to do: save his life.

"Ignacio, in this story the human body is the hawk. It warns us with many signals what we should not eat, but we do not take any notice. When we eat a lot of meat, we are inflated and we cannot sleep well. When we drink too much coffee, we are electrified, accelerated, and we cannot get to sleep. When you eat satvic food your body is at peace and happy, and it thanks you by rewarding you with good health. Learn to listen to the hawk of your body. There is, besides, another kind of food that you do not chew, but that nonetheless contaminates you: television. Television feeds your mind, but unfortunately it fills it with fear, violence, and aggression. If you want to live based on values of peace, happiness, and tranquility, you have to unplug your TV set, or in any case use it to see cultural, pacific programs."

"But if I don't watch the news, how am I going to know what's going on in the world and in the country?"

"Read the newspaper. Watching television is like going to a meal with a fixed menu. It has been prepared by somebody else and it contains what that person likes or regards as good. On the other hand, reading the newspaper is like going to a buffet meal. You have a variety of news items, but you can choose which ones you want to read. Ignacio, be responsible not only for what your stomach takes in but also for what your mind takes in. The search for inner peace is your responsibility. Now go and practice what I have taught you. Come back after three weeks of really applying these lessons."

"But aren't you going to give me a new seed?" asked Ignacio. The master had told him that there were seven seeds. He already knew six of them, and was very curious to know what the last one was.

"Not yet. First you must practice."

CHAPTER EIGHT

Six Seeds in Review

S ix weeks after his meeting with the master, Ignacio had made a serious effort to follow his indications. He had hired a person to teach his wife how to cook a variety of vegetarian dishes. He had stopped eating red meat, but he still had chicken and fish a couple of times a week. Approximately 70 percent of his diet was what the master called satvic food. He had lost weight and now felt lighter and healthier. He had also given up all alcoholic drinks. He had thought he would continue drinking wine, but since his diet was mainly vegetarian, the wine started lying heavy on his stomach, so he gradually drank less and less of it; this seemed to be one of those warning signals that his body could be sending him and that, according to the master, had to be taken notice of.

Ignacio was gradually watching less television also. The first week had been very difficult, because he felt as if there was something missing. He wanted to see the latest news, disconnect his mind while watching television, or simply hear a bit of noise around him. But he had not given in to the pressures of his habit. Now, in the sixth week, he had already become accustomed to not watching television and he was amazed at all the time he had gained to read and to think.

He drank just one cup of coffee in the mornings, because although he had tried to give it up, he simply couldn't manage to wake up and be alert for work without his morning coffee. It was evident that the amount of caffeine he used to consume had accelerated him. He felt a lot calmer now, and was able to meditate much better.

He had finally blocked out his week as the master had recommended. His problem was that he was still not able to deal properly with all the interruptions, to be aware of them. People came into his office, and sometimes he got carried away discussing things with them. He ended up using valuable time that had been set aside for mission-related activities on jobs that were not all that important. Whenever Ignacio realized how long he was spending on interruptions, he politely asked his employees not to distract him, but they didn't like it because habit was stronger than the new policy.

Ignacio had appeared from one day to the next with this strategy of time-blocking to work on the most important things, but in the company they called it the door-blocking policy. Some of the staff accepted the challenge, while others wanted to be listened to every minute, as usual. In reality, the main motivation of those employees was to be near Ignacio, to be recognized, and to feel important, to feel that they had some power. Most of the interruptions were unnecessary and they were usually instigated by his subordinates' egos. Ignacio was in favor of an open-door policy, but he knew that his people should learn to work by themselves. They should make decisions for themselves and interrupt him only when something really important cropped up. He had also taken the time to review all his functions and had delegated the majority of them. He realized that he had been doing an enormous number of routine tasks that took up a lot of his time.

Nevertheless, it was not easy. He felt an emptiness inside him. He saw that whole series of decisions were now being taken in the office without consulting him. This did not make him feel good. He felt that he was no longer important, that his people didn't need him. He realized how his ego was begging him not to delegate, to take the power back. But as well as having his ego addicted to power, Ignacio was truly sad to stop several activities that were not important, but that he enjoyed. They were things he had done all his life, things he did well, but it was really not indispensable that he continue to do them himself. Ignacio realized that blocking his time out implied certain sacrifices, but he was sure that in the long run his investment would pay off handsomely.

He had blocked out some time in the week just for thinking, as the master had advised him, but it was by no means easy. In the office, Ignacio was used to solving problems, taking decisions, and leading meetings. Just thinking took him out of his work habits and upset his ego, which wanted to be moving all the time, directing, being important, and making important decisions. However, he was aware that these spaces of time were helping him to organize himself, to work on pending activities, and above all to anticipate, plan ahead, and innovate for his business.

On the weekends he no longer did office-related work; he spent the whole weekend with his family. At first, this had not been easy for him either. He felt guilty, as he had on those Sundays in his schooldays when he had not done his homework. Not working during the weekend brought upsetting unconscious memories to him. He felt as if he was going to be scolded and punished. But after six weeks it was easier. He was discovering the wonderful experience of playing with his children all weekend. Each time he did so, he ended up exhausted, but with a feeling of love that filled his heart with joy. Now he would not go back to his old ways for anybody; he had discovered a treasure that had always been right there in front of him, but that he had been too blind to see.

After six weeks he felt that he was still not doing things perfectly, but he had made enough progress to see the master again. Ignacio was anxious to receive the last seed. He drove to the master's house. When he arrived, unlike other times when the door was opened to him quickly after he rang the bell, this time nobody answered. Ignacio rang several times, but it seemed that nobody was in. He didn't understand, and he went away frustrated and worried at the same time. He had never had that problem before. He reasoned with himself that perhaps the master had gone out somewhere, or perhaps he had traveled to the provinces. After all, the master was not there just for him; a man like him must have hundreds of matters pending and hundreds of people to attend to. Ignacio was looking forward to seeing him; he wanted to tell him about his progress, but above all he wanted the next seed. He decided to visit the master the following day.

Again, nobody answered the bell. Now he was really worried. It was nighttime, and all the lights were off. He didn't know what to do, whom to ask. He had never remotely imagined that one day the door would not be opened to him. For years he had been visiting the master without any problem. He felt lost, disconcerted, but at the same time frightened. He began to think the worst: "I wonder if something's happened to him?" The house looked empty; there was no sound. "I wonder if he's gone back to his country. . . . But without telling me? No, that's impossible," he thought. Ignacio felt that the master appreciated him a great deal and, as he himself had said, a good master never abandons his disciple. He would never have gone off like that. Ignacio felt upset, but he tried to control himself. To settle down, he began to concentrate on his breathing, and this calmed him. Even now, the teachings of the master were serving him to cope with the pain of the absence of the master himself. He thought that there must be a logical explanation. He went to the house next door and hesitantly rang the bell. A woman of about seventy opened the door. Ignacio said to her:

"Excuse me, ma'am, my name is Ignacio Rodríguez. For some years I have been coming to the house next door to speak with a master from India. Can you tell me anything about him? Do you know whether he has gone away somewhere?"

"Do you mean the man with an orange tunic and white beard, who used to go out walking every morning?"

"Yes, that's him." Ignacio's face lit up, because the woman was obviously able to give him some information.

The woman's expression changed. She became serious, looked down and shook her head. Ignacio interpreted that gesture as saying something very serious had happened to the master.

"Tell me what's happened! What's happened to the master?" Ignacio insisted, with a catch in his voice.

"I'm sorry, I'm very sorry, but your master was hit by a car about three weeks ago, when he was leaving the house. A drunk ran him over and drove away. A neighbor found him bleeding in the street and called an ambulance, but when it came, he was already dead. The neighbor was so impressed because that gentleman had a kind of a smile on his face all the time he was dying."

Ignacio listened to the woman in a state of shock. He felt like crying, but he kept himself under control. The news, hurled at him like a thunderbolt, was too much for him. His legs were shaking and an enormous feeling of revulsion filled him with an unknown kind of fury, an impotent rage, because he had no way to channel it and nobody to take it out on. He suddenly felt cheated, not by the master or by himself, but by something mysterious, something far beyond his comprehension of things. It was not fair, it was simply incomprehensible that things like that should happen. For him, the master was a kind of saint, a magical person who could never die. He was the father and mother he had never had; he felt a deep filial love toward him. Since he had known him, he felt safe and protected by this magical parent. Now that the master was no longer here, what was to become of his life? Who was going to teach him? Who was going to listen to his problems? Who was going to counsel him, transmit words of wisdom, question him? Finally, who was going to show him that disinterested affection, that love that was so compassionate and that had softened and sensitized him? He felt that life was very unfair to him. At the very moment when he was improving and making progress, it had taken away from him his only chance to grow. Once again impotent rage, the feeling that he had been swindled, and also fear filled his soul. He had a knot in his throat, a stifled sob, a horrible heaviness in his stomach, and a constellation of cold drops of sweat on his forehead.

"Take it easy," the woman suggested, with a kind gesture and a somewhat forced smile. "Your friend is resting in peace now."

These words brought him out of his emotional funk. Ignacio told himself: "Wait a minute, here's me lamenting my personal loss, wondering what I'm going to do now, totally self-centered. But I am not thinking of my master. It's true what the woman says, my master is better off now. His spirit is free from physical bonds and limitations, and he is closer to The One."

At first, that sounded to him like a self-imposition, as if there were a little inner voice demanding that he be on guard against his own egoism, but at the same time trying to console him for his irreparable loss. He realized that all his pain did not come from the tragedy that had befallen the master; rather, it was a selfish suffering, focusing on the consequences of no longer having the master at his side. These inner words calmed him a little.

"Look here," continued the neighbor, "they've left the key here with me, so that any friends of his who have things of theirs inside the house can take them out. Do you want to go in?"

Ignacio nodded reluctantly. He didn't know whether he would be able to support the pain of being in the master's room and knowing that he would never see him again.

He opened the street door and went in. Unlike other times when an energy of love and peace had filled the house, this time it felt empty. He remembered the saying he had read so many times as a young man: a house comes becomes a home not when people have finished building it but once they start living in it. The life and the spirit of that house had been the master who lived in it. The garden was drying up and the lawn was yellow. Ignacio opened the front door and went into the room where he had many times before sought the serene, transparent eyes of his master. It was exactly the same as when the master had lived there: the photos of his masters, his bed, his cushions, and his chest of drawers. Ignacio felt a deep nostalgia and an unbearable desire to have his master near.

He sat down in silence to meditate on the cushion where he usually spoke with the master. He had barely started meditating when a thought came to his mind and made him get up from the cushion: "I don't have a single photo of my master." Ignacio looked to see whether there were any on the walls, but there weren't. Then he went to the chest of drawers and opened the first drawer. It was full of letters written in a strange foreign language. "Probably Hindi," he thought. He opened the second drawer and found a plastic document case, like the ones that you get from travel agencies. "The passport," thought Ignacio, "I ought to take the photo from the passport." He opened the case impatiently and found some documents in English belonging to a corporation, apparently British. Intrigued, he continued looking through the papers and found the identification of a business executive, with a photo. He was a person of Indian origin, but dressed in Western clothes. He had short hair, fine features, and was about forty or forty-five years old. He continued looking through the papers and found more photos of the same person in London. One of them in particular struck him. In it, the same person had grown a beard and was sitting on the ground with his legs crossed. He stared at the photo and suddenly realized that it was his master, but many years ago. How come? Had his master been a corporate executive? He had always been sure there was something strange about his master's knowledge of business. His advice had been so valuable because it had fit the situations in the company exactly. But when? How? And why had he entered the world of spiritual things?

Ignacio realized that while he had been with the master, he had been so self-centered that he had never once asked about his life, where he came from, his family, what his personal history was, or simply how he felt. The master had always had the humility not to speak about himself; all his time had been spent serving Ignacio, loving him, and helping him. Ignacio realized that he had taken the master's existence for granted, assuming that it was his right to receive his help and guidance. But he had never even said a simple "thank you, Master." Again the master was teaching him a lesson, even from beyond his material life.

Ignacio left and drove home. In his garden he went to look at his plants, which were, apart from his ring, the only physical souvenirs he had of his master. Looking at his plants he felt like crying; he missed him very much and was not resigned to never seeing him again. He looked at the plants and remembered his transformation as a person. For the first time he was conscious of how much he appreciated his master and needed him. He realized all the master had done for him, all the disinterested help he had given him. A tear rolled down his right cheek, and then he cried for several minutes.

Crying helped him feel better. More than two years had gone by since he had started his conversations with the master, and there in front of him, in the plants, were all the stages he had gone through. He remembered how stupid he had been at his first meeting with the master; how ignorant about his own life and about the road he should take in order to be truly happy. With a smile, he remembered when he had gone angrily to the master because his seed was not growing. Now he was knew that it had been his ego that was angry on that occasion, since it could not bear to think that maybe he had not known how to plant the seed properly.

He remembered how the master had taught him that his present conduct was linked with his past. Then he saw the Sensitive Plant and recognized the role of meditation in his life. Knowing and accepting his past had enabled him to untie his emotional knots, understand his lack of affection, unblock himself, and begin to feel. Meditation, moreover, had enabled him to become immersed in an ocean of inner love, to perforate the depths of his spirit and bring to the surface of each day his inexhaustible reserves of love. Only a few minutes a day of making contact with his soul allowed him to live more at peace and in contact with the divinity.

Then Ignacio looked at the rose. He thought that the master should have chosen a vine instead of a rose. He felt as if his ego was a creeper, closing its tendrils around all aspects of his life. He had it strongly stuck to him and had to make great efforts to pull it off. It was like a weed, difficult to get rid of. His ego was still very much present after these two years, but at least he now knew that it existed, and so he was able to control it. The fourth seed was the mango tree, which represented disinterested service. Never in his life had Ignacio dreamed that he would be giving presentations on spirituality in companies, or caring about other people. But he had never dreamed, either, how wonderful one could feel doing it. The fifth seed was the sunflower, about making ethical decisions. Ignacio had learned to enjoy the feeling of integrity, of union with his soul, and of happiness when what he was doing was in line with the innate qualities of his spirit. The secret of the fifth seed helped him to filter his decisions and acts so as not to stray from that path.

Finally, the last seed he had received from the master was the pine tree, which had helped him more pragmatically. It was clear that he needed it. What was the use of knowing oneself, meditating, controlling one's ego, reflecting ethically, and serving others if one's whole life was disorderly and unbalanced? The sixth seed had enabled him to take control of his life and direct it toward the most important things, namely, to define and organize his priorities.

But what was the seventh seed? Ignacio remembered that he had asked the master for it, but he had not wanted to give it to him. He wondered: if the master had extra-sensory powers and an extraordinary intuition, why had he not had a premonition that he would be run over or that something would happen to him? "Perhaps he never really had powers. Perhaps I was simply idealizing him," thought Ignacio.

Even with such doubts about his master, Ignacio felt frustrated that he had not completed his spiritual training. He felt that he had been climbing a wall on a ladder, in which each rung was a seed. However, on the last rung the ladder had broken. He could not go up any higher and he would never see what was on the other side of the wall.

Ignacio stayed in his garden meditating for a long time. His meditation this time was especially intense. As he concentrated and let go of his thoughts, he experienced a feeling of profound love and unity with everything. The death of the master had brought his spirit to the surface and he felt it in all his being. Gradually, his pain and grief gave way to a sensation of peace and tranquility.

CHAPTER NINE

The Seventh Seed

Three weeks had gone by since Ignacio had learned of his master's death. Now he was meditating longer to try to recover his balance and peace, because he had been deeply affected. Also, he had dedicated himself entirely to service. Ignacio was in great demand as a speaker. His style was both original and entertaining, but at the same time it left listeners with a profound message of change. Since the death of the master, he had accepted three to four speaking engagements a week. Giving the presentations, he felt close to the master. It was a way of paying the master back for everything he had given him in life. When the presentations were over, people would come up to him and shake his hand sincerely and with gratitude. For Ignacio, there could be no better payment that that gesture of happiness or that show of gratitude for helping them to be happier. Service had helped him to free himself gradually from the burden of the master's death, but he still felt frustrated inside that he had not been able to complete his spiritual education.

One night, Ignacio arrived home after a presentation and found a strange envelope on the table. It was a yellow envelope, letter-size, with handwriting that he did not recognize. He looked for the sender's name, but there was nothing written on the back. His heart skipped a beat. Intrigued, he opened the envelope and immediately perceived the typical smell of his master's house, a special kind of incense that he had only ever smelled there. For a few seconds the idea flashed through his mind that his master was alive. He felt panic, hope, and joy at once, but at the same time a lot of uncertainty. He tore the envelope open, his hands tense with nerves, and a few seeds fell to the ground. He quickly took out some sheets of paper that were in the envelope and began reading them anxiously.

> Ignacio, you will have realized by now who is writing you this letter. When you receive it, I will no longer be on the material plane. I have a feeling that my death is near and I have prepared this envelope for you with information about the last seed. I have given precise orders that if anything happens to me, this should be given to you. If you are reading this, it is because that has finally happened. I want you to know that we who meditate for many years, even while we are still in this life, we have the ability to visit the spiritual plane and merge with The One. I had already achieved this merging with The One and, believe me, it is wonderful.

Ignacio could hardly believe his eyes: it was a letter from his master! He went back to the beginning and started to read it again. He wanted to savor and enjoy every word. It was as if they were somehow together again. He was filled with a feeling of immense peace and happiness. His master had not let him down; he had even gone beyond his own death to continue teaching him. After rereading the first paragraph, he continued where he had left off.

> In the first place, I want to tell you that a master never leaves his disciple. Our relationship is forever. I will be with you, on this plane and on the one to come when you finish your material life. You must know that, although I am not physically at your side, my spirit is with you at every moment. For me, the most important thing is that my disciples grow and develop. That is my mission. I was never going to leave you, Ignacio, without giving you the last seed. Believe me that now, for the rest of your life, we shall be closer than before. Before, we were separated by several kilometers. On the plane where I will be there is no separation. We are all one.

Ignacio was filled with emotion and touched by the immense love of his master. His eyes were full of tears and his face had a gentle expression. He continued reading.

> This time I will give you the message of the seed before you plant it. The seventh seed is the seed of freedom, and it is represented by the reed tree. This tree has the peculiarity of being completely flexible. It is able to support hurricane-force winds and can bend until it is horizontal. Its flexibility gives it complete freedom of movement. The only part that is rigid and does not move is its root. The tree has a strong root that fixes it in the ground and serves as its center in order to maintain its

freedom of movement. Unlike the other seeds, the reed tree has many messages of wisdom. Although the word *freedom* summarizes its message, let me explain all that this little tree represents.

First of all, it gives us a message of flexibility. It tells us that we must have the freedom to adapt to the winds of change in life. If the reed were stiff, any strong wind would be able to break it. Your own life is an example of change; look how difficult this change has been for you, but look, too, at the benefits you have received from making these changes. On the material plane, everything changes from one minute to the next, starting with your own body as you grow old. The seasons, the climate, nature, the earth: they all change. Technology changes; businesses and cultures change. Everything changes. The only thing that does not change, Ignacio, is your spirit. You can make ice cubes in many shapes and sizes, and if you leave them out of the refrigerator, they will melt. You can place that water in utensils of different shapes. Finally you can boil that water and evaporate it. Different forms, a series of changes, but water is still water and your spirit will continue to be your spirit forever.

Ignacio, act like the reed; do not be rigid in your life; be willing to change and be flexible. Remember the secret that our true essence never changes and do not be afraid. We human beings are prepared for change. To protect us, our bodies change without any problem. For example, when we are cold, we shiver. This causes friction in our muscles and produces warmth. When we are hot, we sweat. When the water evaporates, we elimi-

nate calories and reduce our heat. As you see, the body
is prepared for change; but unfortunately the mind is
not. To simplify life, the mind creates habits, which are
behavior patterns that have given good results in the
past and that we repeat unconsciously. It is rather like
when we walk in the sand, leaving our footprints there.
If it was a good path and proved to be a good way to
reach our destination, then we will take it again.
Moreover, after we have walked the same path several
times, the sand becomes compressed and hard,
making it even easier for us to go by that path and
giving us greater confidence.

It is like that with habits. They are paths or
behaviors that we constantly use, and they give us
security because they have worked for us before. The
big problem we have is that things change; our goals
change and nevertheless we want to continue using
the same path even though it no longer takes us to
our goal. When a boat is sailing on the sea, it leaves a
wake that marks its path. That path remains marked
for a short time, but, unlike the path on land, it disappears after a while and does not leave any trace at
all. The boat sails through the sea making a new path
every time. This is the challenge for the human being:
to have the courage to create new paths and leave
the familiar routes aside, in order to improve and
grow.

Ignacio put the letter on the table and walked around the
room. What a lot there was to think about! After fifteen minutes, he started reading again.

Many afternoons, while I lived in Lima, I used to sit and
watch people hang gliding along the Costa Verde. Before
they put the equipment on, I used to imagine that if
they jumped off the precipice their destiny would be
simply to fall from the cliffs, pulled down by the force
of gravity. But once they had their hang gliders open,
the rising current of air pushed them up and they were
able to fly wherever they wanted to. It is the same with
the human mind. When it is closed and does not have a
favorable attitude to change, the force of gravity of its
habits takes it along the same paths and that often means
crashing straight into the rocks. Once we open our
mental hang gliders and are willing to admit change,
natural rising currents catch us up in them and make us
grow. But changing and being flexible are not easy tasks,
Ignacio. Your number one enemy will be your ego. It is
the ego that has the most to lose because it feels that it
is the best, the most competent, the most successful.
Changing implies taking the risk of making a mistake
and that makes us vulnerable, which is exactly what the
ego does not want.

Ignacio, every day of your life make an effort to go
above your ego and welcome change. Question your
own behavior patterns, your beliefs, your assumptions,
your prejudices, and even what your perception tells
you. Remember that the sea looks blue from afar, but
when you are near it is transparent. Things are not
always what they appear to be. Do not be convinced by
the obvious, by the familiar; be daring enough to challenge established ideas. Do not be afraid to explore new
territories.

There is a story about some frogs jumping around near a pond. Two of them fell into a deep hole. They both started jumping and trying to get out of the hole, but their attempts were in vain. Meanwhile, the other frogs up on the ground, shouted: "Come on! Come on, girls, you can do it!" However, one frog, seeing that it was practically impossible to get out, decided to give up and die. The other frog continued trying, one jump after another. After a time her friends stopped cheering her on. Instead, they said: "Don't try anymore; there's no point; you're going to die anyway; it's your fate, accept it." But the frog tried and tried again. The frogs up on the ground were in despair. They told her: "Don't be so unfair, don't carry on trying; think of us, we are suffering seeing you there; just die and accept your fate." But the frog kept on trying, until in one of her jumps she was lucky, she grabbed on to the edge of the hole and was able to pull herself up and clamber out. Outside the hole, the frog flopped down on the ground, exhausted, and the others crowded round her and said: "How did you do it? We were telling you not to keep trying anymore; how could you carry on in spite of all that?" The frog, tired out, said: "I am very deaf. . . . I thought that you were cheering me on."

Ignacio, when you change, you will have to be deaf like the frog in the story. Everyone will tell you not to do it like that, it won't work, things will go wrong for you, you'll be sorry . . . and they will do their best to discourage you. That is normal: it bothers people to change their habits, as I mentioned before. But don't pay any attention; go ahead cautiously.

Ignacio stopped reading and spent nearly ten minutes thinking about everything he had read. He felt that of all the lessons, this was the most complete. Then he understood what the master had meant by saying that although he was no longer in this world, they would be closer than ever. He took up the letter again.

> The other message of this seed, Ignacio, is the wisdom of remaining unattached. On the surface, the reed is not attached to anything; it bends before the winds and does not put up resistance as stiff trees do. Under the soil, the reed has its roots firmly attached to the earth. We human beings should be like the reed, free and not attached to anything superficial, to material goods and forms. Our attachment should be only in the depth of our being, in the most important thing we have, in what never changes: in our spirit. To be unattached does not mean that things do not matter to you, it means learning to see the true importance of things. Unattachment means understanding that on this material plane we are all actors in a play put on by The One. Each one of us is playing a part, but everything is unreal. It is simply a play that ends when our life is over. Our true life begins when the play ends. Actors never take the plot of the story to heart and they do not suffer personally from what happens in the play. They are not upset by the problems written into the script or by the crises besetting their character. They know that they are acting and that the play will come to an end and then they will take up their real life.

The challenge for human beings in the play of their life on this material plane is to remember that they are only acting and that the identity of the character they are playing is not their true identity. They are eternal spirits who have come to learn on this plane and take part in The One's game. The One is playing hide-and-seek with us. The One made all creation and then hid in it. He created the scenery, the actors, and the audience, and designed the features of the play. Now we must realize that our life is merely that, a role that we are playing, and we need to find our true identity, that little piece of The One that is in us, in our spirit. The One made creation to experience the happiness of finding Himself little by little, spirit by spirit. That is why when you meditate you feel such great happiness and peace; that is the moment when a little piece of The One finds The One and you feel the nature of your true essence. Ignacio, when the winds of difficulties blow, act like the reed. Do not hold on to anything except your root, your soul. When you are going through difficult times, when you lose something material that you consider important, when circumstances arise that may threaten you, remember that you are playing a part in the play. Do not get upset, do not take it to heart, do not get angry or become negatively and emotionally involved. Keep your distance, stand a little way off like an observer, and remember your true essence.

Remember that your goal in this life is to find that little piece of The One inside you and to live each moment in happiness and peace. That depends on you. You cannot control threatening external stimuli, but what you can do is learn to feel The One at every moment of your life, with your breathing and with meditation. When you are at the beach and the tide comes up, you move so that the sea will not come right up to your beach umbrella. When the tide goes down, you move down nearer the sea, so that you won't have to walk so far to go for a swim. Whether the tide comes up or goes down, you are not worried and you have a great time bathing at the beach. Life is cyclical like the tides. Sometimes we do well, and sometimes not as well as we would wish, but we must learn to have a great time bathing in life, regardless of the tides.

A humble master was walking through the desert. When he came to a village, he tried to persuade someone to put him up for the night, but nobody would do so. So he said with peace and compassion: "The One knows the reason why." He camped in the desert. With him he had a rooster, a donkey, and a lamp. The desert wind blew the lamp away; a cat ate his rooster; and a lion devoured the donkey. Seeing all this, the master said with peace and compassion: "The One knows the reason why." That night some murderous soldiers passed just in front of the master, but because it was dark, and he had no animals to make a noise, they did not realize he was there. They went into the village and robbed and wounded several of the inhabitants. The master said with peace and compassion: "The One knows the reason why."

On the material plane, we human beings are used to having a short-term perspective. We see ourselves immersed in a sea of problems and difficulties, and we feel that we cannot swim. But from The One's perspective, He sees that we are not out of our depth and that if

we would only relax and stretch our legs, we would feel
the seabed firm beneath us. Nothing is good or bad. It is
we ourselves who attach adjectives to things. All circumstances help us to grow, to learn; all circumstances test
our ability to perceive the peace and happiness of the
divinity inside us.

But you must be wondering what to do when you
see the sufferings of poor children, old people who are
sick or infirm, or a friend who has a dire problem. Does
being unattached mean that this does not matter to you,
that you are insensitive to the suffering of other people?
Unattachment has to go hand-in-hand with compassion.
It means understanding that The One is in all things, in
those we perceive as good and those we perceive as
bad, or even as calamities. It means putting yourself in
the other person's shoes and understanding and valuing
that person's suffering, but not suffering it yourself. We
must understand that each human being has a role to
play in the divine drama, he has lessons to learn in this
life, and we must help him lovingly. We must remember
that finally we are all part of The One and that every
human being is in search of the road that will lead us to
Him. Ignacio, you should not be attached to people,
either. When you need a person to fill your life, it is
really because you have a void inside yourself. When
you need a person, you do not love him in the most
spiritual sense of the term, because loving means going
above yourself, above your egocentric needs, and giving
the essence of your soul: love.

There was a blank space in the letter. Ignacio interpreted
this as a suggestion for him to pause and think about what he had

read. After a while he knew that what came next would be a summary of the most important teaching. He hurriedly read on.

They say that there was once a king who was very much attached to his personal goods, his castle, and his jewels, and he lived in fear that they might some day be taken away from him. However, he saw that the poor people in his kingdom were happy and he wondered how it was possible that these people, who didn't even know whether they would have anything to eat the next day, could be happy. He decided to dress as a beggar and discover the mystery. In the village he knocked on the door of a person who very kindly let him in. He was sitting in his little room eating a piece of bread. He invited him to sit down and share his piece of bread. The disguised king asked him: "What do you do for a living?" "I mend old shoes," replied the poor man. "And what are you going to eat tomorrow if you have only this piece of bread?" "Well, I'll eat what I get from my work tomorrow," said the man peaceably.

The king went back to his castle and promulgated a malicious edict. He stipulated that nobody was allowed to mend shoes in the kingdom. He said to himself: "Let's see whether this man will be so calm now." The next day, the king went to look for him again, but he found him with a piece of bread and some cheese. The king in disguise asked him: "I saw that the king had decreed that nobody could mend shoes. What did you do?" "Well, since I couldn't mend shoes, I looked for something to do and I saw some people carrying water. I learned to do it, and offered to help them, and they paid me more than I get from mending shoes. How about that?"

The king went back to his palace, in bad humor. He could not stand the peace and unattachment of the poor man in the village. He promulgated a new law ordering that nobody carry water in the kingdom. The next day he went back in disguise to the house of the poor man, and found him with a bottle of wine, a piece of bread, and some cheese. The king asked him crossly: "But how did you manage this? The king has forbidden people to carry water in the kingdom." The man replied: "I looked around for something to do, I went to the woods and learned to cut trees with the lumberjacks. They saw that I was able to do the work, so they hired me, and paid me very well."

The king was beside himself with indignation. He went to his castle and promulgated another law, ordering all lumberjacks to work for the king as guards. Now he would have him in his hands, thought the king. The next day the king went in disguise to visit the poor man. He found him with a cupboard full of food, all kinds of bread, fruit, cheese, and wine. The king asked him: "But what happened? I know that the lumberjacks went to work for the king and the king pays once a month. How did you get so much food if they haven't paid you yet?" "Well, I worked all day as a guard, but when I went to be paid they told me that they paid everybody at the end of the month. So I thought: What shall I do? And I said to myself: I'm going to sell the steel of my sword and put a wooden sword in its place. With the money, I will buy food. Nobody will notice. When they pay me at the end of the month, I'll replace the sword."

The king thought that now he would be able to catch him out. The next day, the king went to the guards and, pointing to a passer-by, shouted: "Thief! Catch the thief!" He looked at the poor man and ordered him: "Guard, off with the head of this thief!" The poor man thought: "If I draw my wooden sword, they will behead me for selling the steel; if I don't draw my sword, they will behead me for disobeying the king." But since the poor man was always at peace, without attachments, the solution came to his mind as if by magic. He gripped the hilt of his sword and, shouting as loudly as he could, he addressed himself thus: "If this man is a thief, then let my sword behead him. If not, may my sword turn into wood." He drew his sword, held it up, and everyone exclaimed in amazement: "Miracle! Praise be to God!"

The king drew near, appointed the poor man as his prime minister, and said: "Today you have taught me a lesson."

Ignacio, live your life like the man with the sword. Face problems with unattachment and compassion, live your freedom, and have a flexible attitude to life. Like the man in the story, when you live in that way you will be aligned with the divinity and you will always come up with creative answers to your problems.

The lessons have come to an end, Ignacio. Take care of each of your seeds, which are now plants; water them, fertilize them so that they will grow and develop. Take care also of the wisdom of each seed planted in yourself; with patience, fertilize them and water them by practicing and applying their teaching in your life, so that they will grow and bloom in your personal development. I have given you the seeds, now the rest depends

on you alone. Remember your *dharma,* to communicate
with people in business and transmit a spiritual message
to them. Devote yourself to doing that. You will always
be in my heart and I will be with you always.

Your master

Ignacio was awake all night long. He read and reread his
letter, now his most valued treasure. He felt happy and fulfilled.
At last his spiritual lessons were over. He felt whole, fortunate,
integral, and loved by his master.

Nevertheless, it was still difficult for him to adapt to the
physical loss of his master. Two weeks went by during which he
was enclosed in a reflexive solitude, looking at the garden and
with a single idea going round in his head: his *dharma.* There
could be no doubt that his spiritual peace was fully linked with
his mission in this life. Gradually the certainty started to build
in him that his whole life would be a kind of justification with
respect to a central point: to give others what he already knew.
The thought even crossed his mind that now it was he who had
the role of transmitting the wisdom of his master, from a much
more humble position, of course, and using his own resources.
This made him understand in all its magnitude the idea that they
were much closer than before: they were aligned for a single
purpose.

Ignacio thought about the last words in the master's letter
over and over again. He was giving presentations now, and that
was certainly fulfilling his *dharma.* The problem was that he was
reaching a limited number of people with the presentations. He
had received the secret of the seven seeds and he had to transmit this to the greatest possible number of people. "And why

don't I write a book describing my experience with the master?" he asked himself. The title immediately sprung to mind: *The Secret of the Seven Seeds.* He loved the idea. He ran up to his study and switched on the computer . . . but didn't know where to start. Suddenly, after thinking for a while, he decided to start with the incident that had changed his life: his heart attack. So he wrote:

"*Ignacio Rodríguez was anxiously awaiting his turn at the cardiologist's. . . .*"

AFTERWORD

There was once a little boy, curious about spiritual things, who asked his father a difficult question: "Tell me, what is the absolute?" The surprised father affectionately asked him to come out to the orchard with him for a walk around. He picked up an apple, handed his son a knife, and told him:

"Peel it."

The child obediently did so.

"Now open the fruit."

The child did not understand where his father was leading him, but he did what he was told, sensing that something wonderful would be revealed to him.

"Now take out the seeds."

The boy looked at his father somewhat incredulously, but once more he did as he was told.

"Open one of the seeds and tell me what it has inside it."

"There isn't anything, Father," replied the child. "Nothing at all. But what does all this have to do with my question?"

The father, with wisdom and compassion in his voice, told him:

"That 'nothing' that you have found is the absolute; it is something that is everywhere and nowhere at the same time. It is what makes the seed, the fruit, and the tree possible."

This book, *The Secret of the Seven Seeds,* tells of a path of profound personal improvement in which the protagonist, guided by an oriental master, gradually progresses through the message contained in each of the seeds. Although each seed in the book has a lesson for improvement, the main message of the seeds, as described in this little story, is in the encounter with the absolute, the divine, with what is everywhere and nowhere at the same time.

Today we live in a world that does its best to persuade us that happiness and success lie in meeting economic goals and goals of power or prestige, or simply in accumulating the greatest possible quantity of material goods. Human beings are bombarded by ads on the television, the radio, and in the media in general that convince them that they will not be happy unless they possess the products being advertised. It is true that having these products gives a passing feeling of well-being, but then we need, like a drug, to continue filling our emptiness with more and more products in an endless vicious circle. But also, we are subjected daily to a sludge of news that emphasizes everything that is negative (because that is what raises the famous rating), and that fills us with emotions of fear or pain, gnawing away at our tranquility.

True happiness in life comes when we are connected to the absolute, which all of us, from our different traditions, know but call by different names: God, The One, The Spirit. . . . A colorblind person cannot distinguish colors. In the same way, when we are disconnected from the absolute it is difficult for us to realize what the dark things are that we should avoid. This book introduces a path toward the "bright things," toward our positive essence, and toward a life with greater balance, peace and, above all, happiness.

The Secret of the Seven Seeds is designed for people who do not believe in these things—executives and entrepreneurs who, as I myself used to do awhile back, make fun of the human and spiritual aspects of business.

The book is an autobiographic testimony of a personal change, and I hope it can lead even the most incredulous of readers to reflect.

Since this book was published in March 2002, I have had the great satisfaction of receiving comments from people who have stopped to think deeply about their lives, and who have started to meditate or engage in some other spiritual practice. Some have simply become more aware of their own behavior patterns and have taken the first steps along the path to personal improvement. I feel happy to have contributed a drop in the ocean—or the metaphor of each seed—in the lives of these people, and this motivates me to continue writing on the topic.

There is a story about a disciple who ran up to his master and told him excitedly:

"There is an impressive master in the town. I myself have seen how he hammers nails into his feet and scourges himself with a whip, and is able to bear the suffering."

The master listened to him with patience, and with the comprehension of a person speaking with a child, he said:

"My disciple, horses also have nails in their hoofs and are whipped to make them trot faster, but that does not make them masters."

The message of this anecdote is that we must beware of false masters, of those who use phenomenology and the appearance of the mysterious universe of the spirit as a weapon to captivate our egos.

The true road to personal improvement is not miraculous; it is slow and calls for a great deal of perseverance, but it is indeed possible to progress along this road, and your effort will be amply repaid.

What is the secret? Perhaps the answer is in the seven seeds.

QUESTIONS AND ANSWERS

I have used this book as reading material in my MBA classes at the Peruvian University of Applied Sciences. I always ask my students to get together and think up an "intelligent" question about it. I have been asked a large number of questions in my courses, which have led to dialogue. I have selected here the questions that most frequently came up in our dialogues, and that I hope coincide with my readers' curiosity.

The Secret of the Seven Seeds is based on your own life. How much of it is the story and how much of it is true?

Yes, it is mainly based on my life story, although not all the events happened to me. For example, some of the father's mistreatment of Ignacio actually happened to other people. However, I do identify with the character of Ignacio. Most of the ways he puts his foot in it actually happened to me when I was a manager at Cibertec. They often had to change my desks there because of the destructive effect of my bad temper on them. The process of change that the character goes through is real and possible. However, the changes did not all occur in two years as in the story, but over a period of ten years.

Why don't you talk about Ignacio's family?

I had originally intended to talk about the family. I had thought of showing Ignacio's home life, including his marital conflicts and problems with his children. However, I decided to focus on his professional life to make this a personal improvement book addressing the business world. This is a personal improvement book that has a story to give it context, but I never claimed to be writing a novel. Also, if I included the family, the book would be too long, which would make it more expensive and harder to read.

Who is the master?

"The master" is really two people in one. One of them is a highly capable psychoanalyst who helped me personally for many years. A person with life wisdom and a very open mind. Much of his advice is included in the seed of self-knowledge. The second master is a monk who is now on retreat in the Himalayas. I met him in Peru and it was he who initiated me into the practice of Kriya Yoga. He is also a person of enormous wisdom. The unusual thing about this monk is that he is French and about fifteen years ago he was the creative director of Avon France, a cosmetics company. He is very familiar with the two worlds, the Eastern and the Western world, and knows how to build bridges between them.

Why does the master die?

Because I felt it was important to emphasize that at some point we have to stand on our own two feet and not depend on others for our personal development. The master is still alive in real life, but we must be aware that we alone are responsible for our change. Neither masters nor magical gurus will make us into better individuals. They can guide us, and give advice, but the personal change is hard work that depends solely on our own conviction and perseverance.

If meditation is so good, why don't more people practice it?

First of all, in the Western world meditation is not so widespread as in the East. People are not aware of its benefits and advantages, and there are not many centers that teach it. Second, it is like exercise: If there are so many people who know that physical exercise is good for their health, why don't they practice it? The answer has to do with perseverance and the capacity to postpone gratification. Doing exercise is an effort that calls for tenacity and discipline, which are not always in abundant supply. We see the results only after some time, and impatience is a feature of our society. When one begins meditating, one does not immediately feel any benefit. On the contrary, it is boring, unsexy, and tiring. But if we persevere and postpone gratification, we will see remarkable results. I am convinced that meditation is an extraordinary tool for personal improvement. I myself have been practicing it for more than eight years, and it helps me to live a life with more peace, tranquility, and balance.

Did you really leave your body as described in the book?

The facts are real. They came into it at the stage when I was fascinated with phenomenology. I used to buy all kinds of books to learn to leave my body, do astral voyages, balance *chakras,* among other things. It is a stage that many people pass through when they start meditation. It is sexy and attractive, especially when you can tell your friends that you left your body. These are really tricks of the ego that have no meaning. If I commented on it in the book, it was simply to disparage the phenomenological attitude. All these kinds of activities do not lead you to true spiritual development; on the contrary, they take up too much of your valuable time.

How can I deal at depth with the first seed, self-knowledge?

To know oneself is no simple task. It is difficult to know what we are like, especially when the greater part of us is in our unconscious. If we can afford psychoanalysis or psychotherapy, it is very good to do that. We cannot put a price on our happiness; all the money invested to make us happier internally is money well spent. If we cannot afford this, it is important to have an attitude of openness toward self-knowledge. Let us be very alert to the comments of the people around us—our partners, parents, and friends. They see what we do not see. It is easier for them to see our irrational reactions and errors. They can help us to become aware of all our blind zones. Awareness is the first step toward change.

Aren't there any other ways of obtaining inner peace apart from meditation?

Unquestionably there are other ways of achieving inner peace. For many people prayer with devotion is a way. Others find that disinterested service fills their soul. Whichever way you choose, you have to practice it with perseverance. Some people ask me about doing sports, like running. Running can make you feel better physically; it can help you discharge tensions and stress. However, it can hardly give you inner peace or a spiritual feeling.

Where can I find a master who will help me to change?

There is a world organization called Brahma Kumaris (BK). In any search engine on the Internet you can find information about BK. This organization was my first contact with meditation and was most useful to me. They give free courses in meditation and also in personal improvement. It is a philanthropic organization, that is, it does praiseworthy work, disinterestedly, and with great dedication. Another organization is Hariharananda Mission (www.hariharananda.org). This is an organization that teaches the more advanced practice of Kriya Yoga.

Where do you get so many wonderful stories to tell in your book? Are they yours?

I created a few of these stories to illustrate some of the ideas, but the majority of them are ancestral stories from different traditions of the world, such as Jewish, Hindu, and Chinese, among others. I collect stories; they are a source of wisdom that I use when I teach and when I write. After reading this book, you may forget most of its content, but you will never forget the wisdom of the stories.

THE AUTHOR

David Fischman is a civil engineering graduate of the Georgia Institute of Technology, and he obtained his MBA at the University of Boston; both degrees were summa cum laude. He was a founding member of the prestigious Universidad Peruana de Ciencias Aplicadas (UPC), which is now one of the Laureate International Education universities.

An international consultant, he has spent much of his time in recent years researching and teaching leadership topics. Through his workshops he has helped large numbers of executives to acquire the attitudes, skills, and values of personal and interpersonal leadership. He has held conferences and seminars in many countries, including the United States, Mexico, Chile, Panama, and Argentina. He has also been a speaker at several international congresses on leadership. His clients are firms such as Procter & Gamble, Coca-Cola, Banamex, Banco Santander, Banco de Chile, Citibank, American Airlines, Kraft, Merck Sharp & Dhome, and Marriott, among others.

He is the author of books that have sold, to date, more than 260,000 copies worldwide: *El Camino del Líder, El Espejo del Líder, El Secreto de las 7 Semillas, El Líder Transformador,* and *El Líder Interior.*

His column in the Economy and Business section of the newspapers *El Comercio* (Peru), *El Mercurio* (Santiago de Chile),

La Prensa (Panama), and *La Nación* (Costa Rica) is one of the most widely read.

At present he is vice president of innovation and development at UPC, and is a member of the boards of directors of several companies and charitable foundations.